LITTLE BOOK OF THE
BRITISH & IRISH
LIONS

Written by **Paul Morgan**

LITTLE BOOK OF THE

BRITISH & IRISH LIONS

This edition first published in the UK in 2009
By Green Umbrella Publishing

www.gupublishing.co.uk

Publishers Jules Gammond and Vanessa Gardner

Printed and bound in Poland

ISBN: 978-1-906635-45-9

Contents

From The Very Beginning

Rugby teams had been leaving the British Isles since the first Test match in 1871 – when Scotland beat England – and from **1888** when a side travelled to New Zealand and Australia, they have been playing under the broad banner of the Lions. Many of those sides though, at the end of the 19th century and start of the 20th weren't truly representative, drawn from perhaps one or even two of the home nations.

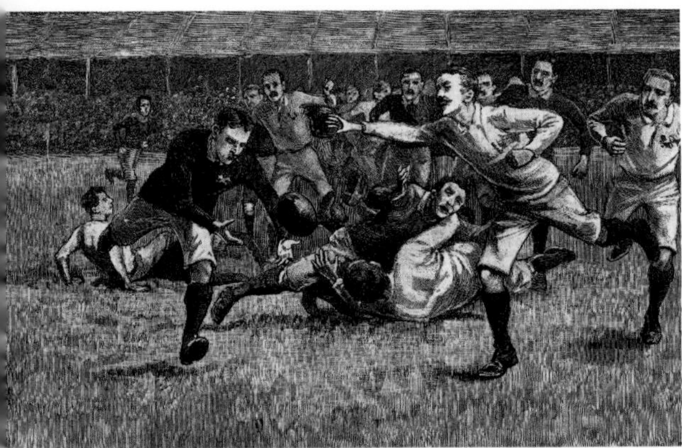

The first official tour by the British Isles Rugby Union Team, selected by a committee from all four Home Unions, was to South Africa in 1910.

But the Lions pioneers first left British shores in 1888, according to the excellent lionsrugby.com website. Rugby players and coaches had barely established the game as an international proposition when they were touring around the world, partly in those days to spread the word of rugby to every part of the globe.

Alfred Shaw and Arthur Shrewsbury's 1888 New Zealand and Australian adventure was a commercial venture and although they were given permission to take the side by England's Rugby Football Union (RFU) it had no formal backing and the side even played some games of Aussie Rules while they were there, games which provided much of the funding. In all, the 22-man team played more than 50 matches, of both codes.

Shaw and Shrewsbury, who got their taste for touring as Test cricketers, led a side that lost just twice in New Zealand on a trip where tragedy befell the party, captain Bob Seddon being killed in a boating accident in Australia.

Once the party returned to England, the rampantly amateur RFU held an investigation into allegations that the players had been paid. Halifax's Jack Clowes admitted he had been paid expenses and was quickly banned from playing rugby. The rest had to sign an affidavit that they had not received financial benefit from the trip.

While the 1888 trip hadn't been welcomed by many of rugby's rulers in the late 19th century, the second trip in **1891**, to South Africa, was a

The early days of the Lions, from their first trip in 1888, through to the First World War, when some of the side's greatest players were lost to the conflict.

1888 Australia & New Zealand
Captains: *Bob Seddon & Andrew Stoddart*
No Test Matches

1891 South Africa
Captain: *Bill Maclagen*
Test Matches: *Won 3-0*

1896 South Africa
Captain: *Johnny Hammond*
Test Matches: *Won 3-1*

1899 Australia
Captain: *Reverend Matthew Mullineux*
Test Matches: Won 3-1

1903 South Africa
Captain: *Mark Morrison*
Test Matches: *Lost 1-0, with two draws*

1904 Australia & New Zealand
Captain: *David Bedell-Sivright*
Test Matches: *Won 3-0 v Australia*
Lost 1-0 v New Zealand

1908 New Zealand & Australia
Captain: *AF Harding*
Test Matches: *Lost 2-0 v New Zealand, with one draw*

◀ New Zealand were one of the first opponents of the Lions.

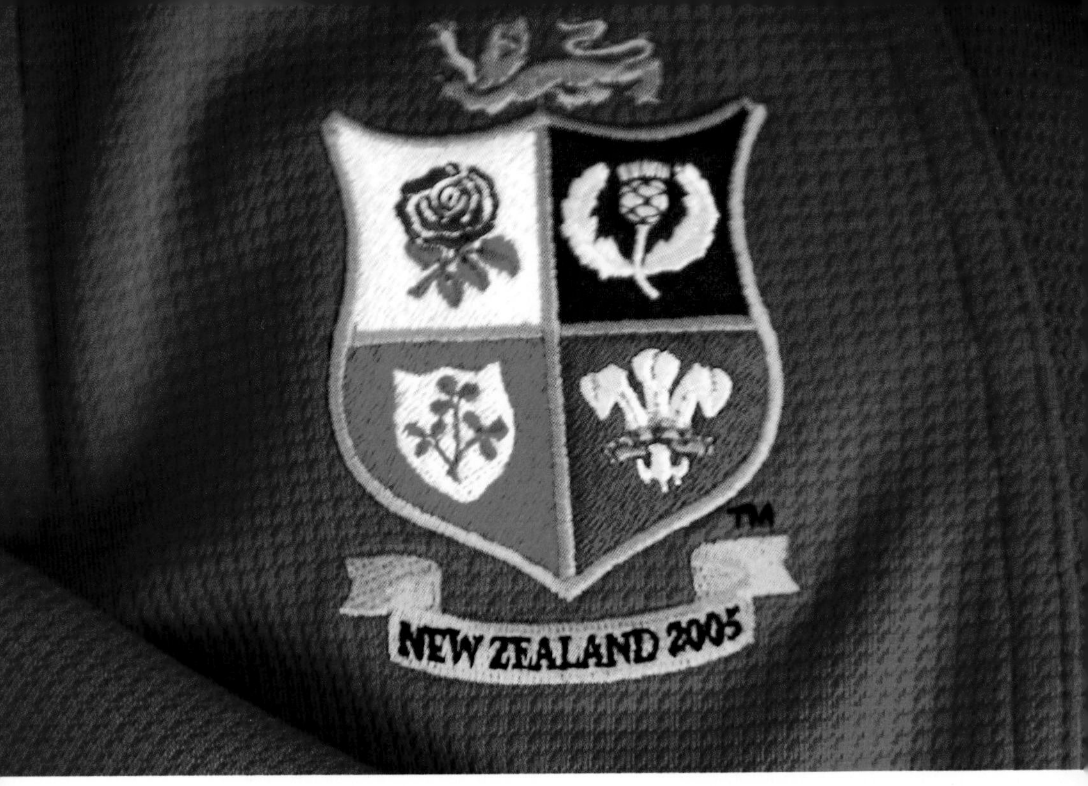

different affair with official backing, even underwritten from a financial perspective by Cape Colony Prime Minister, Cecil Rhodes.

The team in fact travelled under the auspices of RFU, ensuring that the trip, although backed by the English, wasn't representative of the four home nations. English players dominated the 22-man squad, even though it contained four Scots, including captain and wing, Bill Maclagen.

Unlike in modern times, the South African side was far from world champions, and as a rugby nation, only emerged on the international scene with any force in 1906 when Paul Roos brought his side to Great Britain, being called Springboks for the first time.

The 1891 tour was more about establishing rugby as a sport in South Africa, and the drubbings the South Africans received in all games clearly only served to inspire the home nation! So hammered were they on the tour, South African teams only scored one point. The Tests were won by the British side, 4-0, 3-0 and 4-0.

The Lions also left more than a passion for rugby behind them, presenting the Currie Cup, a silver trophy presented to Griqualand West, and even today it is still regarded as South African rugby's biggest domestic prize.

The 1891 tour was the last when any British side had their own way in South Africa, although they still managed to win the next series in **1896**, 3-1, losing the last Test in Cape Town.

The side was certainly taking on more of a home nations hue, with players from Ireland joining the party. The Irish, who were becoming a major force in the home nations championship, demanded their inclusion after winning two Championships and a Triple Crown in the previous three seasons.

The British and Irish side were still pioneers, and although they lost the final Test, they had a remarkable record in their provincial games, winning all 17 matches and scoring 204 points. These tourists based their winning formula around a formidable pack that was inspired from No 8 by Ireland's Tommy Crean. Fred Byrne set a record on the trip that lasted until 1960, amassing 100 points. Alf Larard was the man to go down in the folklore of South African rugby history, scoring his country's first try in international rugby as they won the final Test at Newlands 5-0.

The **1899** tour to Australia was the first to include players from all four home nations, although the side was still not under the auspices of a Home Nations Committee, as it is today.

Of the 21 players who left England, the squad included seven internationals, two Scottish, two Irish, two English and one Welsh.

Having provided South Africa's first Test opposition in 1891, the Lions performed the same role for Australia in 1899.

Still unbeaten in Test series terms, these 1899 Lions returned home having won 3-1, even though they lost the first

◀ Lions players can come from any of the four home unions.

▲ An All Blacks shirt from early in the 20th century.

Test in Sydney.

Captained by Blackheath's Reverend Matthew Mullineux, the side didn't actually play "Australia" as the country was still 18 months away from Federation, instead taking on a side made up of players from the two rugby states of NSW and Queensland.

The game of rugby was first played in New South Wales as early as the 1860s, but the arrival of the Lions side gave the sport a huge boost. It took near neighbours New Zealand until **1903** to make the trip across the Tasman.

In 1903 the Lions travelled back to South Africa and with the nation on the verge of discovering a golden generation of players, the Lions suffered their first defeat, as part of an epic three-Test series.

The first two Tests in 1903, in Johannesburg and Kimberley, were drawn with the South Africans winning the third, Cape Town, 8-0, as the Lions were taken to their limits on a trip when they only won half of the 22 matches in total.

Like the Lions of today this side was a true representation of the best that the British Isles has to offer. England captain Frank Stout and his counterparts with Ireland (Alf Tedford) and Scotland (Mark Morrison) were in the pack while the exceptional Reg Skrimshire was the key Welshman in the backs.

The 1903 manager, Johnny Hammond, was starting to become a Lions legend of Willie John McBride proportions, figuring in his third successive trip.

The Lions had clearly got a taste for touring at the turn of the century and while today's Lions tour every four years, they only waited 12 months this time, leaving the UK again in **1904**.

The 1904 tourists broke new ground, playing Tests in both Australia and New Zealand for the first time.

Rugby union was still the breeding ground for league in Australia and with the prevalence of Aussie Rules in the country, the Lions were too strong, sweeping them aside 3-0 in Tests. But in New Zealand, where the game was starting to take a grip, it was a different matter, the Lions losing their only Test there, in Wellington.

In selection terms these Lions regressed slightly, as the party was selected by invitation, so it wasn't as strong as it could have been, led by Scot, David Bedell-Sivright, who had been a key man in 1903.

Like the so successful 1971 and 1974 Lions the 1904 party had a set of impressive Welsh backs at its core. Perhaps the most famous of the lot, Gwyn Nicholls was unavailable, but William Llewellyn, Percy Bush, Rhys Gabe, Tommy Vile and Edward Morgan were present.

Bush came to international recognition on the tour, ensuring the Lions hammered Australia, although the task was altogether different, and much tougher, in New Zealand, where the home side had a pack based on the 2-3-2 formation, later outlawed.

By the time the Lions travelled again four years later, in **1908**, New Zealand had begun their drive to become the pre-eminent side in world rugby, and under AF Harding the Lions played three Tests, against New Zealand, losing two and drawing one.

▲ The Lions beat South Africa 3-0 on one of their first tours, in 1891.

This trip, called by some an Anglo-Welsh squad, brought a change of colours. With the Scottish and Irish unions declining to be involved, an Anglo-Welsh squad headed for Australia and New Zealand, red jerseys with a thick white band reflecting the combination of the countries.

The writing was on the wall for this team as they struggled in Australia, so went to New Zealand fearing the worst, and it came as they could only manage nine wins in their 17 games. Although the Lions managed to draw the second Test, 3-3, they were hammered 32-5 and 29-0 in the other two internationals!

Establishing The Lions

▶ As rugby took a back seat, a First World War recruitment poster was produced using rugby union players.

▶ The Springboks team before the third Test against the touring British Isles team in 1924 at Port Elizabeth, South Africa.

In **1910**, the Lions embarked on their last tour before the First World War, and did it in style, actually being involved in two separate trips, for the first and only time in their proud history, to South Africa and Argentina.

In the years before and after the First World War the Lions travelled to two countries, South Africa and Argentina.

1910 South Africa & Argentina
Captain: *Dr Tom Smythe (South Africa)*
Captain: *John Raphael (Argentina)*
Test Matches: *Lost 2-1 v South Africa Won 1-0 v Argentina*

1924 South Africa
Captain: *Ronald Cove-Smith*
Test Matches: *Lost 3-0, with one draw*

1927 Argentina
Captain: *David MacMyn*
Test Matches: *Won 4-0*

The squads that travelled to South Africa and Argentina were completely different, with Dr Tom Smythe leading the trip to South Africa and John Raphael to Argentina.

South African rugby was getting stronger with every season and they were developing their team into one of the most formidable in the world, so it is probably no surprise to discover that the Lions were well beaten, although their results were marginally better than the result obtained on their last trip, in 1908. At least this time they won a Test match, even if they lost the series 2-1.

The tour to South Africa took in 24 matches and although the Lions started well with consecutive wins over South Western Districts and two Western

Province sides, they were ultimately outgunned in the three-month trip, losing the first and third Tests, although they did manage an 8-3 victory in the second, in Port Elizabeth.

The 1910 tourists were considered the first to truly represent the four home unions of England, Wales, Scotland and Ireland, and with 26 players it was the biggest squad in Lions' history.

Smythe's squad introduced dark blue jerseys, white shorts and red socks as their playing kit.

The visit to Argentina proved again the Lions' pioneering nature, as the game was the country's first Test match, 37 years after the first rugby match of any kind was played in Argentina.

The rugby wasn't anywhere near

as hard as it was for Smythe's side in South Africa; the Raphael squad did much to spread the gospel of rugby.

The Argentina party was largely an English monopoly but the presence of three Scots in the squad, lifted it into Lions history.

In Argentina, managed by Oxford University and RFU stalwart RV Stanley, the tourists encountered only limited opposition, scoring 213 points to 31 and winning the Test 28-3, in Buenos Aires on 12 July.

The **1924** tourists, the first to travel after the war to South Africa, were the first to set out from our shores under the title of the British Isles Rugby Union team, and legend has it they were the first side to officially pick up the moniker of Lions.

It seems the side, which played in blue shirts, were given the nickname from an emblem on their ties, but however it was added into rugby's folklore it stuck!

◀ The Lions team leaving for a tour of South Africa aboard the *Edinburgh Castle*, June 1924.

Being called Lions didn't make it any easier to win a Test series though, and they lost the series 3-0, managing one draw.

Skippered by legendary England forward Ronald Cove-Smith, these 1924 Lions collected the unwanted record of being the least successful British and Irish visitors to South Africa, winning nine and losing nine of the 21 matches they played. In the middle of the tour they even went through a run of eight matches without a victory.

Rugby in the British Isles was still struggling to recover from the ravages of the War, while the game in South Africa was coming on leaps and bounds, the 1924 Springboks setting course for one of the most successful periods in their history.

At a time when no replacements were allowed, the 1924 Lions also struggled with a mounting injury toll on South Africa's hard grounds, and in some of their games they even struggled to find 15 fit men to play. This led to forwards playing in the backs and some backs taking their turn up front.

In 1924 the side wore dark blue jerseys, the same colour shorts and red socks.

These Lions were defined by their bravery, managing to secure a 3-3 draw in the third Test in Port Elizabeth. The resilience of Cove-Smith's men was confirmed at the end of the trip as they signed off from the two-month tour around South Africa with an 8-3 victory against Western Province in

▶ Mr Robertson Gibb, (left) manager of the Union Castle Line and Mr Cove-Smith, captain of the Lions rugby team sailing for South Africa, 1924.

Cape Town.

Three years after returning from South Africa, in **1927**, the Lions made their second trip to Argentina and this time there was no mistaking this team from Britain and Ireland as they carried the same emblem of the four Home Unions that is worn today and were managed by former RFU president James "Bim" Baxter, on his first tour.

Captained by Scotland lock David MacMyn, the 23-man party included 11 internationals, as well as four players who would also tour Australia and New Zealand three years later: Carl Aarvold, Roger Spong, Jimmy Farrell and Wilfred Sobey, the last going as vice-captain.

Invited by the River Plate Union and bankrolled by donations and fundraisers, the 1927 Lions were way out of their opponents' league and rattled up 295 points while conceding just nine.

Four of the matches were Tests, all of which were won by MacMyn's men, by margins of 37-0, 46-0, 34-3 and 43-0. Despite the one-sided nature of the contests, the tourists drew large crowds and left the hosts with both a handsome profit and a renewed appetite for the game.

2
PERSONS.
24
PER

◀ Members of the British Lions touring team practising scrum half passing during a training session.

Locking Horns

▶ Prince Alexander Obolensky, a tourist in 1930.

Long before the advent of round the world commercial flights, the **1930** trip took the 29 tourists five weeks to reach New Zealand by passenger boat, heading to Auckland via the Panama Canal.

In the years before the Second World War, Lions tours took off, embracing Tests against New Zealand, Australia, Argentina and South Africa.

1930 New Zealand & Australia
Captain: *Doug Prentice*
Test Matches: *Lost 3-1 v New Zealand*
Lost 1-0 v Australia

1936 Argentina
Captain: *Doug Prentice & Bernard Gadney*
Test Matches: *Won 1-0*

1938 South Africa
Captain: *Sam Walker*
Test Matches: *Lost 2-1*

There was a decidedly Welsh vein running through the squad. Harry Bowcott was one of the stars of the 1930 trip and Lions rugby certainly agreed with the outside-half as when he died in December 2004, at 97, he was the oldest surviving Welsh rugby international and British and Irish Lions Test player.

On the Lions tour he was still a student at Cambridge and with college team-mate Carl Aarvold, formed a destructive force for the Lions, scoring four tries. Bowcott played in 16 of the Lions' 21 games in New Zealand, scoring six tries, and four of the six official games in Australia, including the Test defeat.

The 1930 Lions were still in blue

◀ South Africa breaking out with the ball during the 1938 Lions tour.

jerseys, but this time they caused controversy because of the clash with their hosts' famous All Black. It meant that New Zealand agreed to change for the Tests and the All Blacks became the All Whites for the first time.

But even though they were forced into new jerseys New Zealand were no less formidable. After they lost the first Test to the Lions in Dunedin they roared back to win the series 3-1, the last Test in Wellington secured 22-8.

The game was still developing across the world and New Zealand's use of a 2-3-2 scrum formation, with a "rover" at the back came to an end in 1930, but not before it had been used one last time to defeat the Lions. The tactic led to a complaint from the Lions manager James Baxter, at the end of the trip, and the International Rugby Board acted, banning it from the game. This led to the three-man front row we see today, being adopted for all levels of the game.

But that ruling came too late to help the 1930 tourists, who were also hampered by selection issues and when they got to New Zealand a spate of injuries. England captain Wavell Wakefield was one of a number of

▶ South Africa's Danie Craven breaks through the Lions' defence.

players from the British Isles unable to make the trip. Nevertheless the Lions upset New Zealand in the first Test; a late try from Jack Morley, created by Wales full-back Ivor Jones saw them home by three points.

That Dunedin victory was as good as it got for the 1930 Lions in the Test matches, although they did win 19 of their 27 matches on the whole tour. The length of the trip proved too much for the Lions in the end, as they went to Australia on the way home, losing their one Test match in Sydney 6-5, and to New South Wales, 28-3.

Between the tours in the 1930s to New Zealand and South Africa the Lions journeyed, in **1936**, to Argentina, the last time the tourists would make the trip to South America.

Unlike the southern hemisphere superpowers, Argentina was still developing as a rugby nation, the Lions proving far too strong for their hosts.

The only Test match – in Buenos Aires – was won easily, 23-0, and the Lions proceeded to win every one of their 10 games, scoring an impressive 399 points, and conceding just 12. Many of the matches were considered no more than exhibitions, the Lions only conceding one try on the whole trip, against Belgrano in the run-up to the Test.

The 1930 captain, Doug Prentice, was co-captain this time, along with his England team-mate Bernard Gadney and while the games were won with ease the trip proved to be a good breeding ground for future Lions.

One of the British game's legendary figures, Prince Alexander Obolensky was on the tour. Obo as he was known the length and breadth of every rugby nation around the world was killed in the Second World War, but not before he had left an indelible mark on the game, scoring two tries on his England debut, as they beat New Zealand, 13-0, for the first time in their history.

The last tour before the Second World War, in **1938**, saw the Lions returning to the homeland of one of rugby's two superpowers: South Africa.

The Lions had fared badly on their recent trips to South Africa and this time they had to take on one of the most impressive Springboks sides in history, as they had just beaten both New Zealand and Australia away from home.

As the Lions had done on their last trip to South Africa, in 1924, they lost

the Test series, although this time instead of a clean sweep the Springboks only won 2-1, the tourists emerging victorious from the third and final Test, 21-16, in Cape Town.

Managed by Major BC Hartley and captained by Ireland forward Sam Walker, these Lions put the pride back into the jersey, scoring more points than any previously and causing a huge shock in that final Test, winning 17 of their 24 matches on the whole trip.

Stars like full-back Vivian Jenkins, hooker Bill Travers, scrum-half Haydn Tanner, and back-rowers Laurie Duff and Bob Alexander were at the core of this Lions effort that surprised their hosts.

The second – and deciding Test – went down in legend as the Tropical Test when the Lions were forced to play in heat approaching 100° in Port Elizabeth. Needing to win to stay in the series, Duff scored the Lions' try but his side finally wilted to lose 19-3.

The 1938 Lions ended on a high with a final Test side that contained eight Irishmen. Trailing 13-3 at half-time, the Lions fought back to win by five points, their first victory in a Test match in South Africa since 1910.

The Lions Roar

The first golden era of the British and Irish Lions arrived in the 1950s, and although they still may have struggled to win a Test series in either of the powerhouses of New Zealand or South Africa, the men in red established respect and the love of the rugby world in the period after the Second World War.

On their first trip after the war, the Lions avoided a repeat of the 1930 colour-clash controversy in **1950** by adopting the famous red kit they still wear today. When Karl Mullen's 1950 Lions ran onto the pitch for the first time, they did so with red jerseys, white shorts and green and blue socks, combining in one the colours of all four nations. More than ever they were clearly representing the four rugby nations of England, Wales, Scotland and Ireland.

In the 1950s the Lions donned their famous red jerseys and proved they could thrill crowds on the world stage.

1950 New Zealand & Australia
Captain: *Karl Mullen*
Test Matches: *Lost 3-0, with one draw, v New Zealand*
Won 2-0 v Australia

1955 South Africa
Captain: *Robin Thompson*
Test Matches: *Drew 2-2*

1959 Australia, New Zealand & Canada
Captain: *Ronnie Dawson*
Test Matches: *Won 2-0 v Australia*
Lost 3-1 v New Zealand

◀ Karl Mullen, the skipper in 1950.

Supporters from all over the world fell in love with the Lions in the 1950s because of the way they played the game.

They kicked off the decade in New Zealand and although they only managed one draw (9-9 in Dunedin in the first Test) they won friends the length and breadth of the two islands.

Back in the British Isles, Ireland and Wales had both just won Grand Slams and Wales were discovering a rich seam of players.

Known as The Friendly Tour, because of the way these Lions conducted themselves on their trip, they were the last tourists to leave British and Irish shores by boat!

The Lions concept meant that players like Ireland outside-half Jackie Kyle and Wales wing Ken Jones could take the field together, both later named in the list of the New Zealand Rugby Almanac's five players of the year.

Welsh centres Jack Matthews and Bleddyn Williams were acclaimed, but it was up front where the battle-hardened All Blacks gained the upper hand.

Under the leadership of Ireland's Grand Slam captain Karl Mullen, they led 9-3 until the final minutes of that first Test in Dunedin, only for All Blacks captain Ron Elvidge to score a try and rescue a draw for New Zealand.

◀ Flying wing Ken Jones goes over the line in New Zealand.

◀ One of the great Lions, Cliff Morgan, breaks the Spingbok defence.

Staying in the south island for the Tests the Lions went down 8-0 in Christchurch and 6-3 in Wellington, before moving back to the north to lose 11-8 in Auckland, all three defeats by tiny margins.

In Auckland, Ken Jones struck one of the great Lions tries, a sensational length of the field score.

The 1950 Lions proved their pedigree with a quick trip to Australia on the way home, where they won 19-6 and 24-3 in their two Test matches, scoring five tries in the second game.

In **1955** the Lions and South Africa completed one of the most fascinating series in the history of rugby and after four Test matches, that swayed to and fro nothing could separate these two great sides, drawing their epic series 2-2.

The backdrop for the trip was South Africa's Grand Slam on their own tour of Britain and Ireland in 1951-52.

South Africans fell in love with the 1955 Lions not just because they took their beloved Springboks to the wire, but because of the way they played the game.

There was a spirit amongst the 1955 Lions that all touring sides tried to replicate.

Led by formidable Irish second row

▶ Lions captain Ronnie Dawson and All Blacks captain Wilson Whineray lead out their teams at Dunedin, July 1959.

Robin Thompson and his Northern Irish team-mate, Jack Siggins, the Lions shocked the rugby world in the first Test, in Johannesburg.

In front of a staggering 100,000 people, the Boks took the lead before the Lions stormed back for a pulsating 23-22 victory that set up the series perfectly.

In Jo'burg tries from Cecil Pedlow, Jeff Butterfield, Cliff Morgan, Jim Greenwood and Tony O'Reilly created the platform for the win, although it was only sealed by a missed injury-time conversion by South Africa full-back Jack van der Schyff.

The series advantage held by the Lions didn't last long as a proud Springbok side bounced back in the second Test in Cape Town, winning 25-9. The Lions felt the Springbok backlash in the second Test, with winger Tom van Vollenhoven scoring a hat-trick in a revenge mission.

But the men from Britain and Ireland ensured at least a share of the series with a 9-6 win in Pretoria, where England's Jeff Butterfield scored a try and kicked a drop goal at Loftus Versfeld, in front of 45,000 people, with Cliff Morgan as captain.

▲ The Lions rugby team before their summer tour of Australia and New Zealand, May 1959.

The Lions managed that crucial victory with only 14 men. Long before the advent of substitutes, Reg Higgins had to go off with an injury and couldn't be replaced.

The third Test was the first international match played at the famous Loftus and Wales hooker Bryn Meredith recalls the tour, saying: "That third Test was a real war of attrition. Both sides knew that, with the series poised 1-1, this was the vital game.

"We had to hold on in the first Test to win by a point, but were forced to play for half the game with only 14 men. That third Test at Loftus was one of the hardest games of rugby I've ever had to play.

"Our backs were generally regarded as our strength but, on that day at

Loftus, I'm proud to say that our pack, containing six Welshmen, stood up to the Springboks and came out on top. We had a hell of a party that night."

The 2-1 advantage gained by Butterfield's brilliance wasn't enough though as South Africa showed their pedigree by taking the final Test, 22-8 in Port Elizabeth.

In that final Test the Lions led 5-3 at half-time, but tries from Greenwood and O'Reilly weren't enough as South Africa broke free in the second half, to share the titanic series 2-2.

So revered were the 1955 Lions that around 5,000 people turned up at the airport to see them leave and on the way home they stopped in Kenya, to beat an East African XV 39-12 in Nairobi.

They were loved the length and breadth of South Africa because of the way they embodied the spirit of rugby.

In their midst were some of the legends of the European game. Wales outside-half Cliff Morgan, the man who carried on the traditions of the famed Welsh outside-half factory was pulling the strings, while Englishman Dickie Jeeps was his partner at half-back. Outside those two, the gem of Tony O'Reilly, a teenager on the tour, scored a staggering 16 tries.

Between O'Reilly and his half-back heroes were the English centre pairing of Jeff Butterfield and Phil Davies.

But those backs couldn't have prospered in the intimidating atmosphere of South African rugby without a hard-nosed pack, containing great players like Bryn Meredith, Rhys Williams and Jim Greenwood.

▼ Bleddyn Williams.

▶ Jeff Butterfield, one of the stars of the 1955 trip.

Morgan, christened "Morgan the Magnificent" by the South African newspapers, was one of the players who was fervently committed to providing the Lions with an off-field reputation as strong as their on-field persona, charming the South Africans and leading the squad's legendary Glee Club in song, at every opportunity.

The 1955 Lions' commitment to attacking rugby ensured the side's best record in South Africa since 1896.

"It seems like a big film and I was an actor in it," said Cardiff wing Gareth Griffiths, when speaking about the tour in 2007. "It was marvellous. We were well sought after, the South Africans liked us and the rugby was great.

"Being a Lion in South Africa was a bit like dying and going to heaven – everything I ever wanted to achieve came together in a fantastic four months."

The Lions also played two matches against Rhodesia in the middle of the tour, winning both of them.

The **1959** Lions, under the captaincy of Ireland hooker Ronnie Dawson, took on a mammoth trip, touring Australia, New Zealand and Canada, fairing far better in their games against

▶ Tony O'Reilly of the Lions fends off D J Davison of the All Blacks at Wellington in 1959.

the Wallabies than the Kiwis.

Like the 1955 side, the 1959 Lions were a very talented group – they were just unlucky to come up against Wilson Whineray's teak-tough New Zealanders, who triumphed in the Test series 3-1.

In Australia at the start of June it was however a different story as the Lions warmed-up for their trip across the Tasman by winning both Tests, comfortably, in Brisbane (17-6) and Sydney (24-3). They also won three out of four of their provincial matches, passing the 50-point mark in the opener, against Victoria, when they won 53-28.

A large number of the 1955 tourists went again and their philosophy of a game plan that revolved around attack was again at the core of the side.

This strategy, with Tony O'Reilly, Jeff Butterfield and Dickie Jeeps left from the 1955 backline, brought an impressive four tries in the first Test, in Dunedin, but not the victory as they lost, agonisingly, 18-17. That day they succumbed to the almost unerring kicking of "Super-boot" Don Clarke.

In the first Test, Wales centre Malcolm Price led the way with a brace of tries, Tony O'Reilly and England's fleet-footed wing, Peter Jackson, also crossing the Kiwi line.

The 1959 Lions had agreed to a punishing provincial schedule as well as the four Tests, and although they won all but two of their non-Test matches they took their toll – on a trip that lasted four months – as the tourists were forced into eight changes for the second Test, in Wellington.

Another close run match went the wrong way, as far as the Lions were concerned, New Zealand winning 11-8 – Clarke was again the thorn in their side, this time not just with the boot as he scored a try as well.

The third Test and the series went the same way, in Christchurch, as the Lions lost 22-8.

But these Lions were made of stern stuff, using the provincial games as a platform to take the final Test, in Auckland, 9-6. They recorded four successive victories, against New Zealand Juniors, The Maori, Bay of Plenty and North Auckland on the road to Eden Park, and it gave them the momentum they needed.

Tries from Bev Risman, O'Reilly and Jackson got them home in Auckland as New Zealand replied with two penalties

from the irrepressible Clarke.

It was fitting that O'Reilly and Jackson should be on the scoreboard again in that final Test, as their partnership will never be forgotten in the history of the Lions. O'Reilly ended the tour with a record-breaking 22 tries, Jackson pushing him all the way with 19.

The remarkable O'Reilly also ended the decade having scored more tries for the Lions in Tests than anyone else, with six from 1955 to 1959, a record that still hasn't been overtaken.

Tough Times

▶ Stompie van der Merwe and hooker Bryn Meredith leap high during a lineout.

The Lions won just two Test matches in the 1960s as they lost heavily to both South Africa and New Zealand. They were battered but remained unbowed.

If the 1950s was a golden era, the Lions struggled to build on their reputation in the following decade, struggling through the 1960s, suffering defeat after defeat to South Africa and New Zealand.

They failed to win a Test match against either the Springboks or the All Blacks in the entire decade, although they did manage a couple of victories, in 1966, against Australia.

In **1962** they travelled back to South Africa and instead of the agile backline that had defined the 1950s the Lions placed too much reliance on a giant pack, which got them close to parity in the Test series, ensuring they in fact drew the first encounter with the Springboks, in Johannesburg, 3-3. In that first clash legendary Wales wing Ken Jones struck with 10 minutes to go, with a 60-metre try through the South African defence, to tie the scores.

1962 South Africa
Captain: *Arthur Smith*
Test Matches: *Lost 3-0, with one draw*

1966 Australia & New Zealand
Captain: Michael Campbell-Lamerton
Test Matches: *Won 2-0 v Australia*
Lost 4-0 v New Zealand

1968 South Africa
Captain: *Tom Kiernan*
Test Matches: *Lost 3-0, with one draw*

The Avril Malan Springboks who had toured Europe in 1961 had set new

standards, losing just one game, their last, to the Barbarians, so the Lions knew that trying to beat them in their own backyard was a huge task, a year later.

And although the 1962 Lions will be remembered for losing the Test series 3-0, with that one draw, they were far from disgraced on their trip, despite the final Test hammering, winning 16 of their 25 games on the whole trip, which included victories over Rhodesia, East Africa and South West Africa at the start and finish of the trip.

The big pack of forwards signified their intentions, but the squad still possessed some world-class players behind the scrum. Players like Richard Sharp, Ken Jones and Dewi Bebb joined Dickie Jeeps, who is still the Lions' second most-capped player in history, with 13 Tests to his name.

Despite this talent they lacked creativity according to Clem Thomas in his masterful *History of the British and Irish Lions*.

"They had no one, especially at half-back to light the spark," said Thomas.

"The solid Gordon Waddell and Mike Weston, who played in all four Tests at centre, but were often pressed into service at fly-half, were more strong tactical kickers than sharp runners, which is what was required on the hard grounds of South Africa."

The Test series was finally lost in the third international, when the South Africans took an unassailable 2-0 lead with an 8-3 victory in Cape Town.

And it was only in the final Test when the Lions finally collapsed losing 34-14, in front of a capacity crowd in Bloemfontein.

The 1962 trip was the first of six tours for perhaps the most famous Lion of them all – Willie John McBride. Born in County Antrim in Northern Ireland, McBride toured with the British and Irish Lions once as manager, once as captain and four times as a player. From 1962 he went on to skipper the side on their unbeaten 1974 tour of South Africa, becoming manager of the 1983 Lions on their trip to New Zealand.

McBride was called out of Lions retirement in 2001, when he was asked to present the players jerseys before their first Test victory over Australia.

The scrum-half in 2001, Rob Howley, explained the impact McBride had made on Lions rugby saying: "I could feel the hairs on the back of my

◀ Bryn Meredith attempting to get the ball away from Popeye Strydom during a game in Port Elizabeth, July 1962.

▶ Mike Campbell-Lamerton powering his way past the Australians.

neck growing as he spoke. It was a masterstroke from the management. Willie John is regarded as the greatest Lion of all and to hear his words so close to kick-off was inspirational.

"Willie John's words were special and I am so glad we carried it off for everyone involved."

The Lions had to wait until 2005 to find a worse tour to New Zealand than the one endured in **1966**.

In many ways the 1966 Lions were unlucky as they clashed head-on with an All Blacks side on the verge of the greatest winning run in the history of Test rugby.

Between 1965 and 1969 New Zealand went on a world-record breaking run of 17 consecutive Test match wins, the four against the Lions showing just how good those All Blacks were.

For many people the 1966 tour, which was the first to have a coach in the shape of John Robins alongside manager Des O'Brien, was the low point in Lions' history, but that ignores the abilities of the All Blacks at that time.

The four Test defeats in New Zealand were a long way from the minds of the Lions at the start of the tour when they went unbeaten through eight games in Australia, including 11-8 and 31-0 victories in the Test matches, against the Wallabies. The slim victory, in Sydney, attracted a crowd of 42,303, a then record for a rugby union match in Australia.

Of course, the 1966 Wallabies were a shadow of the Australia side we see today but 202 points in those eight games was good form with which to head across the Tasman Sea.

But the Lions were left in no doubt about the magnitude of their task in New Zealand within the first few weeks, as they only won three out of their first five provincial games, the first defeat, 14-8 to Southland.

When defeats to Otago and Wellington followed, the Lions travelled to Dunedin for the first Test more in hope… but even that hope quickly evaporated as they were crushed 20-3.

That loss did galvanise the Lions as they proceeded to win their next five tour matches, before a much-closer second Test, in Wellington, which they lost 16-12.

Embarrassment at being the worst Lions to tour New Zealand turned to virtual humiliation on the way home

as they lost 8-3 to British Columbia, before ending the trip on something approaching a high as they beat Canada 19-8 in the final match.

Mike Campbell-Lamerton proved a controversial choice as captain, as he hadn't even led Scotland in the previous Five Nations Championship. He was ultimately left out of two of the Tests.

Vivian Jenkins *The Sunday Times* rugby correspondent remembered the tour, saying: "There is also no question of whether a team enjoyed itself on tour. I regret to report that, while nearly every one of the touring party said he would love to come back to New Zealand as an ordinary visitor, not one of them (and this was confirmed by the tour manager, Des O'Brien) wanted to return to play rugby.

"Competition taken to the extreme, as it is in New Zealand, produces things that, to our own players, are not worth the ends involved. Dirty play is one of them and there was more than enough of this on tour.

"Kicks on the head, which necessitate stitches, or broken noses from stiff arm tackles, do not come under the heading of hard play, to which no rugby man objects. Instead

◀ Tom Kiernan.

◀◀ The skipper in 1962, Arthur Smith.

they are just plain dirty. No doubt we will be accused of squealing, the usual New Zealand comeback, but the only alternative is to stay silent and respond in kind, and what kind of a game does that make rugby?"

Wilson Whineray, the New Zealand captain had a different view on the Lions' troubles. He said: "It is clear in retrospect that the Lions' decision, made early in the tour, to play the All Blacks up front was wrong.

"They suffered from battling to narrow wins, or not winning at all, and the spectators suffered from watching dreary rugby."

The Lions did at least leave something worthwhile behind in New

Zealand… a large pot of cash! The final Test attracted a crowd of 58,000 to Auckland's Eden Park, bringing in record gate receipts for any match in New Zealand of £43,000.

The Lions of the 1960s showed some indication of the glorious rugby that was to follow in the 1970s, although the **1968** side had little in the way of Test results to show for their trip to South Africa, save a 6-6 draw in the second Test in Port Elizabeth.

Coached by Ireland legend Ronnie Dawson and captained by Tom Kiernan, the 1968 Lions were, like their compatriots of 1962, not as bad as their Test record shows, as none of their three defeats to South Africa were by big margins.

They certainly couldn't have blamed full-back Kiernan for their defeats as, apart from one try, he scored all the Lions' Test points on the tour. Kiernan's total of 35 was a new points-scoring record for an individual in Tests, in one tour, and stood until Gavin Hastings overtook it in 1993.

Kiernan's record was one to remember, while Wales prop John O'Shea had one to forget, becoming the first Lion to be sent off for foul play, after O'Shea threw a punch. He wasn't the first Lion to be dismissed, that unwarranted record falling to England's David Dobson in 1904 who was sent off for abusive language.

Some of the players who captivated the rugby world in 1971 and 1974, emerged on the 1968 trip but one of the most gifted, Barry John, failed to last even the first Test after injury struck. John's absence through a broken collarbone allowed Mike Gibson to become the first injury replacement in any Test match, in the history of the game, but also thrust a world-class centre into a jersey where he was far less comfortable.

With John in the driving seat the Lions started the tour so well, with six successive victories, so losing the first Test 25-20 was a body blow to their hopes of a series victory.

Although the Lions continued winning their provincial matches, the Tests slipped away from them after they drew the second Test, in Pretoria, 6-6, the Springboks took an unassailable lead with an 11-6 victory in Cape Town. But any thoughts that this was a poor Lions team were disputed by their results outside the Tests, where

◀ Springboks player Dawie de Villiers in action, 1962.

they won 15 out of 16 games, which included a win over Rhodesia.

These Lions were, in fact, more respected inside South Africa, where it was clear they pushed the Springboks far closer than they were ever given credit for.

The legendary Dr Danie Craven, known in South Africa as "Mr Rugby", described their impact. "The Lions were a good team, well prepared and well coached. How near they came to beating us in the series is something we are inclined to overlook," said Dr Craven.

"It is true that we beat them convincingly in the first and last internationals, but in both those matches the important turning points came our way.

"The Lions gave us grey hairs and it was a great achievement to have beaten them in the internationals."

The South African public clearly agreed, as even with the series won, 60,000 of them packed into Ellis Park for the final Test, as the Springboks won 19-6. The injury problems that beset the touring party were demonstrated by the fact that the Lions played Gordon Connell in the No 9 jersey, their third scrum-half replacement.

◀ Dickie Jeeps gets the ball away under pressure from Brian Harrison.

Rugby From Heaven

A golden generation of players from Britain and Ireland landed in the rugby world in the early 1970s, giving the Lions an unprecedented level of success, with back-to-back series victories against New Zealand and South Africa.

The only debate that rages in the minds of fans of Lions rugby is which of the 1971 or 1974 sides was the better?

The British and Irish Lions uncovered an incredible set of players in 1971, as they travelled to New Zealand under legendary coach Carwyn James.

1971 New Zealand
Captain: *John Dawes*
Test Matches: *Won 2-1, with one draw*

The answer is probably unattainable as both sides (which contained some of the same players, of course) were equally brilliant, in their different ways.

The **1971** side will forever be remembered as Carwyn's team as they were led by the unforgettable Welsh coach Carwyn James, a progressive and intuitive man, who embodied the spirit that every successful Lions tour needs.

As a player, James was in direct competition with Cliff Morgan, only winning two Wales caps, but his role as a coach means that he is still discussed in hushed tones in Wales today as a pioneer.

James had a much-heralded column in *The Guardian* for some of his career and in those pages revealed the core of his philosophy.

"The boring, unthinking coach continually preaches about mistakes.

▲ The team that toured New Zealand in 1971.

The creative coach invites his players to make mistakes. Adventure and error go together. I loved Lewis Jones's way – 'I may concede two, but I'll score four!' he explained.

"Successful man-management is no more than demanding your team's 'cocky blighter' remains outrageously full of himself, and ensuring your morose grumbler can moan as much as he wants. Express yourselves, I tell my teams, not as you would at the office, but as you would at home."

James stayed as a thorn in the side of the All Blacks, coaching Llanelli to victory over New Zealand, at Stradey Park Llanelli in 1972, but it was his role with the 1971 Lions that gave him a legendary reputation in the rugby world.

When James died in 1983, Barry John remembered him, saying: "From my point of view, he had the finest

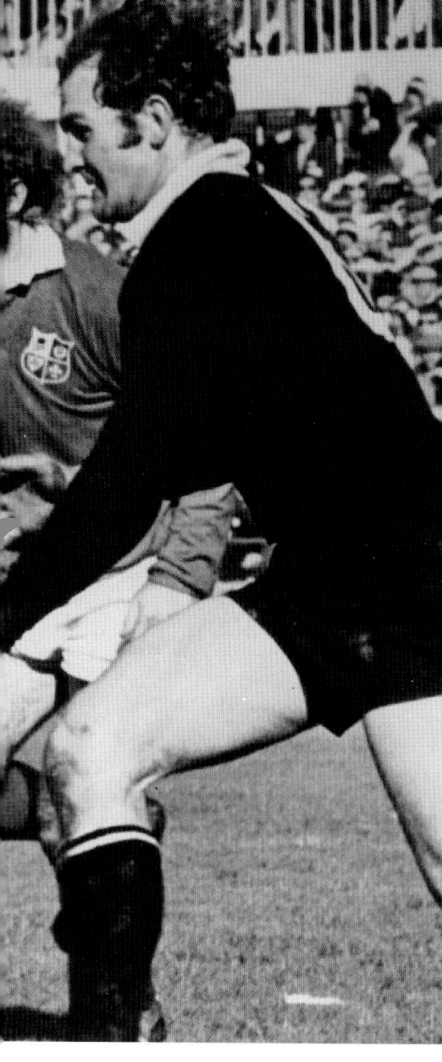

◀ Gareth Edwards storms through the All Black line, supported by John Taylor.

rugby brain I have ever known. He was brilliant at man-management and at analysing play. His great virtue was that he always had time for others, asking players their opinions and judgements."

The Lions had never won a series in New Zealand before – or since – so the achievement of the 1971 team could hardly be exaggerated. And not only did they win, but they won well, suffering just one defeat in New Zealand, in the second Test in Christchurch, during their 24 games in the land of the long white cloud.

Bizarrely they did lose one other match after leaving the British Isles, in one of two warm-up matches in Australia, against Queensland. That defeat caused Queensland coach Des Connor to make one of the worst predictions in rugby history, suggesting these Lions were the worst ever to be sent to New Zealand! How wrong he was!

Coach James led a Lions party bristling with Welsh players, after they had just won a Grand Slam, and their abilities underpinned the effort in New Zealand, although key players from England, Scotland and Ireland made the 1971 side so impressive.

E
14

Alongside James was perhaps the most under-rated member of the team, manager Dr Doug Smith, the former Scotland wing.

Captain John Dawes remembers his influence. "Doug was a master of man-management and discipline, he never lost his cool, he could sense if one of his men was upset and we knew the key to his room was available for any Lion who wanted to get something off their chest," said Dawes in *The Sunday Times*, giving exceptional insight into how a successful Lions squad is blended into a team of winners.

And of James, Dawes adds: "Even the way he ate a meal was graceful. He was steeped in the culture of Wales and exceedingly well read. His preparation and insight were masterful, his analysis of the New Zealand players was outstanding and enabled us to nullify their strengths."

The Welsh spine of the team started with James and was continued by his captain, Dawes.

The influence of the Principality could be felt in almost every part of the team, ensuring players like Gareth Edwards, Barry John, Gerald Davies, JPR Williams, Mervyn Davies, John Bevan, Derek Quinnell and John Taylor would never be forgotten.

But this was not just a Welsh achievement with David Duckham and John Pullin of England, Willie John McBride and Mike Gibson of Ireland and Scots Ian McLauchlan and Gordon Brown, playing key roles.

Past Lions teams had packs to match the All Blacks, but in 1971 they had a golden generation of backs, who could capitalise on the possession won by McBride and his forwards. That pack also needed to repel the physical challenge set down by every New Zealand based side they faced. A number of times, particularly when they faced Canterbury, it went too far, turning into violence and dirty play.

Successful Lions tours always have a good record outside of the Test matches, and in 1971 one of the crucial wins was over the powerful Wellington side, who they beat 47-9.

"It was a special afternoon," captain Dawes said "and we entertained the crowd and showed them the handling game at its best. It stopped the loudmouths in mid sentence and more important, it both astonished and worried the New

◀ Players leap for the ball at Eden Park, Auckland, August 1971.

Zealand rugby fraternity."

It is almost invidious to pick out individual players in a team of teams, but for one it was their last Lions tour, and no one who thinks of the 1971 Lions can do it without thinking of "The King", Barry John.

A broken arm had ruined his 1968 trip, but in 1971 he established himself as one of the greatest talents the game has seen, scoring 30 of the Lions' 48 points over the four Tests.

Described as rugby's first superstar, John scored a record 191 points in his 17 matches in the whole 1971 tour, bringing his own brand of mercurial rugby to the Lions, scoring in every game he played in. John even sat on the ball during one game against Hawke's Bay, to protest at the home team's foul play.

John retired aged 27, but like George

▶ Mervyn Davies feeds Gareth Edwards, with Gordon Brown in support.

▼ Barry John being pursued by Tane Norton of New Zealand.

9

▶ Flanker Fergus Slattery in action during the 1971 tour to New Zealand.

STE

▶ John Dawes, the captain in 1971.

Best in football, left so many great memories those who saw him were glad he was around for the short period he was – the 1971 Lions tour was perhaps his greatest memory.

Alongside John was the man who many describe as the greatest player the game has ever seen, Gareth Edwards.

The first Test, in Dunedin, set the tone with six Welshmen – and Mike Gibson as the only Irishman – in the backline. Dominated for much of the match the Lions still emerged 9-3 winners, Sandy Carmichael scoring a try, with John kicking the crucial points and also tormenting New Zealand full-back Fergie McCormick.

The All Blacks tied the series with a 22-12 victory in Christchurch, even though a stunning 50-yard try from Gerald Davies set the Lions on their way, along with the boot of John. The defeat ended the Lions' run of 15 successive wins in New Zealand, although Davies's second try on that day allowed him to join an elusive band of Lions, joining Carl Aarvold (Christchurch, 1930) and Malcolm Price (Dunedin, 1959) as the only three Lions players to score two tries against New Zealand in one Test match.

The Lions ensured they couldn't lose the four-Test with a decisive win in Wellington, 13-3, John scoring a well-worked try after an initial break from Edwards.

But a drawn series was never going to be enough for this special group of players and they became the first Lions to win a series against the All Blacks when they drew the final Test in Auckland, 14-14.

A try from English No 8 Peter Dixon – who went on the tour before being capped by England – ensured the sides were locked at 8-8 at half-time.

In the second half a penalty from John and a thumping 45-metre drop goal from JPR Williams got the Lions the draw they needed, All Black Laurie Mains tying up the scores with his own penalty.

As rugby writer Clem Thomas remembers: "The draw was enough for the Lions to go home as heroes, and it was a good party!

"By becoming the first British team to win a major series abroad in the 20th century, these 1971 Lions had become the greatest, and had struck a vital blow for the cause of British rugby. Carwyn James had vindicated the new move to coaching and silenced the doubters."

The Glory Continues

If Lions fans thought they had been spoilt in 1971, it was a case of "you ain't seen nothing yet" as the **1974** side went to South Africa and won an epic series 3-0, with one draw, ensuring legendary status for another set of men in the famous red jerseys.

With many of the players who had won the Lions' first ever Test series victory in New Zealand three years earlier, the 1974 Lions went with more than hope to the Republic but few thought they could achieve their incredible feat of 21 wins from 22 matches, a 14-14 draw in the final Test match in Johannesburg, spoiling their perfect record.

One of the ultimate Lions, Willie John McBride, was the captain and a catalyst for a sensational tour that brought an incredible 729 points, including 107 tries.

From one incredible squad to another, in 1974 the Lions travelled to South Africa to complete another set of records.

1974 South Africa
Captain: *Willie John McBride*
Test Matches: *Won 3-0, with one draw*

◀ Willie John McBride leads his team during the tour of South Africa, 1974.

McBride ended his career with 17 Lions Test caps; four more than any other player and the manager in 1974, Arthur Thomas, remembers the man from Ballymena.

"The captain was another exceptional man, and all the credit for the team's success goes to him and his great ally, Syd Millar (the coach)," said Thomas.

"His outstanding qualities as a player and a man are so well known that I can never adequately describe them in print.

▶ Preparing for a scrum.

"He was literally worshipped by the players, not only because of his own courage and strength of commitment, but because they saw in him all the things they would like to be.

"He shielded them, nurtured them and, above all, inspired them. He shirked nothing, and was that rare breed, a natural leader of men."

There was an undercurrent of violence on this tour. Before the Lions left Heathrow they met and resolved not to be intimidated by the South Africa players, both in provincial games and Test matches, as they knew they would face a barrage of physical intimidation.

The Lions' response was the infamous "99 Call". Devised by McBride, he would call "99" if any Lion was in physical danger and it allowed for a "one in all in" approach in response, based on the theory that the referee couldn't send them all off!

McBride, who was on his fifth Lions tour, told the players never to take a backward step. "We've learned over the years in South Africa and New Zealand that you must always stand up to anything that is thrown at you," said McBride.

That pledge was helped by the set of rock solid forwards that left Britain, many describing them as the greatest players in rugby history.

Men like front rowers Ian

McLauchlan, Bobby Windsor and Fran Cotton probably greeted McBride's words with a knowing smile. The man who could intimidate guys like them hadn't been born, so McBride needn't have feared them shirking from any level of physical confrontation.

In the management team McBride had the perfect foil in coach Syd Millar, just like the 1971 side had

Carwyn James.

Millar was crucial because pulling together the best players from four nations had proved beyond some of the best minds in the game. He may have played 10-man rugby when he needed to, but he also released his backs on as many occasions to dazzle the Springboks.

As manager Arthur Thomas wrote in his end of tour report, Millar set the tone.

"Syd Millar motivated and inspired the players to great heights and helped them realise their potential," said Thomas.

"He was the perfect choice and the perfect companion. His happy nature belied the steel in his character and whilst he was very much a players' man, he was broad enough to chide them if they stepped out of line.

"He had a clear vision of what was required to win, and to hear him analyse and evaluate tomorrow's problems at the team talks on the eve of the game was an experience. He was so simple, so articulate and yet so masterful. No team has gone on the field better prepared."

The spirit ensured the 1974 Lions enjoyed themselves on and off the field and japes they got up to in a succession of hotels were as legendary as their exploits on the field.

After one particularly boisterous evening in one hotel the door to McBride's room had been smashed down and a number of items had been damaged.

The hotel manager burst into McBride's room and informed the skipper that the police had been called. The Irishman thought for a minute, took a puff of his famous pipe and said, staring the hotel manager straight in the eye; "Will there be many of them?"

Coach Millar also tried to forge an unbreakable bond between the midweek side and the Test XV, as he saw both sides as crucial to the Lions' Test chances.

Any great team is defined by their reserves and when you consider great players like Tony Neary, Chris Ralston, Mike Burton, Sandy Carmichael, Andy Ripley and Tommy David featured in the list of back-up players for much of the tour you get an idea about how good the Test team must have been!

The 1974 Lions had a huge effect on everyone who saw them and after Jake White coached South Africa to their

◀ Fran Cotton, Willie John McBride and Mervyn Davies grapple for the ball against the Springboks.

◀ Gareth Edwards scores a try against Natal.

World Cup win in 2007 he talked about how much they had meant to him.

"I've never been involved against the Lions or with the Lions but it's something I've grown up with as a young South African," said White.

"In 1974 the Lions came to South Africa and everyone still talks about that Lions team. It's something in rugby that is unique, something in rugby that you get one chance to do."

There was no sojourn in another country on the way this time and the Lions hit the ground running, beating Western Province 59-13 in their first game, Phil Bennett converting all seven tries, and building up a run of seven successive victories before the first Test in Cape Town.

Their run of wins proved to be the perfect preparation as Bennett kicked three penalties, while Edwards grabbed a drop goal to see them home 12-3, in the first game against South Africa.

Gareth Edwards was at the height of his considerable prowess on this tour, his form leading McBride to describe him as "the best scrum-half I have seen or am ever likely to see".

Barry John's retirement left Phil Bennett, another Welshman, alongside

▶ Ian McGeechan and Dick Milliken with the Lions mascot in South Africa.

Edwards, with the unenviable task of stepping into the most famous shoes in the rugby world.

But luckily for the Lions the old Welsh Fly-Half Factory produced another genius in Bennett and he dazzled in South Africa, scoring in each of the four Tests.

The Springboks didn't help themselves as the selectors panicked after the first Test, making eight changes, and suffering an even bigger defeat, 28-9 in the second, a record for any Lions Test team.

Bennett ended the tour with an impressive 130 points and no one present will forget his try in that second Test; a 50-metre effort that included some of his trademark sidesteps.

The second Test victory was even more impressive as it came on the high veldt, in Pretoria, where the Lions had to cope with the problems of altitude, after winning the first clash at sea level.

JJ Williams, the great Wales wing, showed his world-class ability with two tries in the victory; centre Dick Milliken, Bennett and the "Broon of Troon", lock Gordon Brown, also going over. JJ ended the series with a record-equalling four tries.

South Africa only got marginally closer to the Lions in the third and decisive Test, in Port Elizabeth, losing this one, 26-9, and the series, but not one Springbok would take any consolation from the closer margin.

The 100 per cent record was dented in the fourth and final Test, in Johannesburg, when the Springboks restored a tiny amount of pride with a 13-13 draw.

The Lions were convinced they had won that one as well, open-side Fergus Slattery crossing the line, only to see the referee rule that he had been held up.

But they joined the record books as only the third Lions side to score 10 tries in a Test series, joining those who went to Australia in 1904 and South Africa in 1955.

Despite that disappointment in the final game the 1974 Lions were left to reflect on a record-breaking, incredible tour, that few people predicted and no side could ever emulate. After the trip, centre Ian McGeechan, who would go on to coach the Lions, said the players had developed a bond that would stay with them for the rest of their lives. Anyone who saw the 1974 Lions, even from a distance, would agree.

Following The Legends

▶ Bobby Windsor, a member of the famous Pontypool front row kicks ahead against Bay of Plenty.

Most rugby historians feel nothing but sympathy for the **1977** Lions. After the exploits of 1971 and 1974, it was a case of "follow that" and unfortunately the side that travelled to New Zealand in 1977 struggled, finally losing the series 3-1.

The tours in 1977, 1980 and 1983 had to follow in some of the most famous of rugby footsteps... and they found the going tough.

1977 New Zealand
Captain: *Phil Bennett*
Test Matches: *Lost 3-1*

1980 South Africa
Captain: *Bill Beaumont*
Test Matches: *Lost 3-1*

1983 New Zealand
Captain: *Ciaran Fitzgerald*
Test Matches: *Lost 4-0*

The 1977 Lions mustn't be remembered as distant losers as they missed drawing the Tests series by one point, losing the final Test of four 10-9 in Auckland.

Led on the field by Phil Bennett and coached by 1971 captain, John Dawes, the squad had 18 Welshmen, when replacements were taken into account, reflecting a golden era for the country in the Five Nations Championship.

Bennett privately doubted his ability to lead the Lions to New Zealand and revealed in his book *Everywhere for Wales* that he regretted accepting

▲ Brynmor Williams gets the ball away before being tackled by Dave Henderson of Wellington.

the armband. "I should never have accepted the captaincy of the Lions in 1977," he revealed, after a tour that was remembered by many who went on it by the atrocious weather that winter in New Zealand.

"I have spent many a wistful hour thinking of what might have been achieved had the leadership gone to someone far better equipped than I to deal with the all-engulfing pressures of a three-month rugby expedition."

Bennett though had nothing to be ashamed of as his Lions won 21 out of 25 matches in New Zealand, only losing outside the Tests once.

After the successes in 1971 and 1974, there also wasn't much evidence of an inferiority complex at the start of this tour as the Lions kicked off with eight straight wins, including a 60-9 victory over King County-Wanganui, but a 21-9 defeat to the New Zealand Universities in the game before the

▼ Captain Phil Bennett battles for the ball against Waikato.

▶ Bobby Windsor on the charge during the match against the NZ Juniors, 1977.

first Test gave them an idea of what was ahead.

Up front the Lions had the ability to match the All Blacks, but behind the scrum – where scrum-half Gareth Edwards had decided not to tour – they struggled to compete with New Zealand in the four Test matches.

In the pack, the front row in particular of Fran Cotton, Peter Wheeler and Graham Price, would compare favourably with any the Lions had sent out in their glorious history.

A great day though, reminding people of their exploits in 1971, arrived for the Lions in the second Test in Christchurch, when a sensational JJ Williams try, and three penalties from Bennett, inspired the men in red to an exciting 13-9 victory.

The game was marred by acts of violence but the way Welsh legend Terry Cobner stepped up and took control of the Lions forwards will never be forgotten.

Although they lost the third Test in Dunedin 19-7, the Lions missed a golden opportunity to make more history and square the series in Auckland by the slimmest of margins.

That final result, losing just

▶ Terry Cobner giving a half-time team talk, 1977.

▶▶ Bill Beaumont jumps at a lineout during the tour match against Western Province, July 1980.

10-9, was achieved after the Lions lost four of their best players in the run-up to the game; Derek Quinnell, Brynmor Williams, JJ Williams and the heartbeat of the pack, Cobner. With them the 1977 Lions could have been lauded in the same breath as the other sides from the 1970s.

The Lions even led 9-3 at half-time in the final Test, with a try and penalty from scrum-half Dougie Morgan, but they couldn't hang on.

The myth of the 1977 Lions being a poor team was probably founded by their trip home, where they lost 25-21 to Fiji, but it was the Test results in New Zealand, rather than this final game that defined the side as one of the better Lions parties to travel to the land of the long white cloud.

Wales may have been the great breeding ground for Lions in the 1970s, but as a new era dawned so did a new and powerful side, England, under the leadership of Bill Beaumont kicking off the decade with a rare Grand Slam in the Five Nations.

Beaumont, who made his Lions debut in 1977, was the obvious choice as captain in **1980**, under coach Noel Murphy, and he took

nine more Englishmen with him, although Wales still dominated the party with 16 players.

Beaumont became the first Englishman to captain the Lions, since Douglas Prentice 50 years before.

It was a tough tour for the Lions in more ways than one. They didn't know it at the time but due to the political problems in South Africa and the opposition to the abhorrent Apartheid regime, the Lions wouldn't return until 1997.

Those political problems did raise

their head on the tour, with players refusing to travel and demonstrations greeting the Lions, while the games were crammed into a far shorter space than ever before. The Lions were asked to play 18 games in 10 weeks, and this inevitably led to the British and Irish side suffering a catalogue of injuries.

Moves by the UK Sports Council and other bodies to call off the tour were rebuffed, but they travelled in the middle of a political storm.

In the end it was the injuries that ensured the 1980 Lions returned home without the spoils. They started in the first minute of the first game, when Stuart Lane tore his ligaments.

The toll went on, and as Clem Thomas remembers in his definitive history of the Lions: "Consequently we saw three fly-halves, five centres and four wings.

"It was the first Lions party to take a doctor with them. In Dr Jack Matthews,

◀ John Beattie and Alan Phillips rush for the ball during the match between the Lions and Griqualand West.

▼ The Lions take on Griqualand West at the De Beers Stadium, July 1980.

▶ Members of the Western Province squad look on as Ollie Campbell kicks at the goal.

▶▶ Ciaran Fitzgerald goes for the ball in the match against New Zealand at Eden Park, July 1983.

a Welsh Lion of 1950, they had the right man, and my word, how he was needed! In fact, these Lions could have done with a team of doctors."

Despite the problems, the 1980 Lions lost just three of their 18 games on the tour, but unfortunately all three games were in Tests so the series was lost 3-1.

The series defeat was signalled in the first Test as they were outscored five tries to one in Cape Town, only the boot of Ireland outside-half Tony Ward, which contributed a record 18 points, kept the score respectable at 26-22.

The Lions went down 26-19 in the second Test and lost the series in Port Elizabeth, but only just, 12-10. A Bruce Hay try put the Lions ahead in Port Elizabeth and even though their forwards were not in the ascendancy, the Springboks fought back, Naas Botha earning the victory, converting Gerrie Germishuys's try.

The Lions had to wait until the final Test, in Pretoria, to record a win against South Africa, 17-13. With the victory, it ensured the 1980 Lions avoided becoming the first to suffer a whitewash in South Africa and the only Lions side to win a fourth Test in the Republic.

Prop Clive Williams was an

unlikely first half try scorer and after the Springboks pulled the score back, second half tries from Andy Irvine and John O'Driscoll (the uncle of 2005 captain, Brian), with a final kick from Ollie Campbell getting them home.

The final victory was nothing more than the Lions deserved, captain, Beaumont, being chaired off at the end to reflect their pride in the win.

If there were positives to come out of the 1977 Lions defeat in New Zealand, it was hard to find any six years later, in **1983**, when they returned to the land of the All Blacks, suffering a 4-0 whitewash in the Test matches, conceding a record 38 points in the final match, in Auckland.

It was the first time the Lions returned home without a Test win since 1966, the side captained by Ireland's Ciaran Fitzgerald, coached by Jim Telfer and managed by Willie John McBride suffering from the off, as they lost only their second game on tour, 13-12 to Auckland.

History will reflect a controversial selection as captain in Fitzgerald, because although he had led Ireland to a share of the Five Nations Championship in the same year, many considered both Peter Wheeler of England and Colin Deans of Scotland to be better hookers.

But to lay the blame for the defeats at Fitzgerald's door would be invidious and even their final tour result, winning 12 out of 18 games, wasn't bettered by the Lions who went to New Zealand, under Sir Clive Woodward, in 2005.

At the time the southern hemisphere were pulling clear of their British and Irish cousins, a fact that was reflected in the first World Cup, which arrived in rugby union four years after this tour, won easily by New Zealand.

Premier Lions historian, the late Clem Thomas explains: "The results of this tour again mirrored the decline of British rugby in the 1980s and, without any profound analysis, the brutal truth was that the All Blacks were a far better team and the Lions were outplayed in the Test matches.

"For all that they were a splendid bunch of men, who accepted their vicissitudes and worked hard for elusive success, and Willie John (McBride), who was perhaps too protective of his team at times, kept their morale up and ensured they soldiered through to the end."

Lions stars on this tour were few and far between although everyone will

◀ Pass master Roy Laidlaw, spreads it wide.

remember the contribution of players like tight-head Graham Price, flanker Peter Winterbottom, and outside-half Ollie Campbell.

The power of the All Blacks lay in their pack as they picked the same set of eight forwards for the whole Test series, so in many ways it was to the Lions' credit that they held them so close in the first Test, losing just 16-12.

The Lions' lack of firepower was however illustrated in Wellington, in the second Test, where they failed to score against New Zealand for the first time

◀ Ollie Campbell clears the ball upfield as New Zealand's Wayne Smith closes in.

since 1950, resulting in a 9-0 defeat.

The Lions bounced back to outscore New Zealand two tries (from Roger Baird and John Rutherford) to one in the third Test, in Dunedin, but still lost, this time 15-8 to ensure the series slipped away.

It is a shame for the 1983 Lions that they managed to let the All Blacks dominate the final Test, in Auckland, losing 38-6 and giving the tour a far worse hue than the team warranted; the All Blacks' biggest win against a British side in their history.

Back To Winning Ways

The longest gap between Lions tours (from 1983 to 1989) since the Second World War was caused by the Apartheid political regime in South Africa. Opposition to Apartheid led to the Republic being banned from international rugby, and missing both the 1987 and 1991 World Cup in addition to the planned 1986 Lions tour.

It was a long time coming but the Lions finally had a winning side to follow those in 1974.

1989 Australia
Captain: *Finlay Calder*
Test Matches: *Won 2-1*

1993 New Zealand
Captain: *Gavin Hastings*
Test Matches: *Lost 2-1*

The Lions did play on British soil instead, in 1986, as a side was assembled to play an International Rugby Board XV at Cardiff Arms Park, the overseas side winning 15-7.

The six-year wait for a tour ended in **1989**, as the Lions came from behind to win a Test series against Australia. Although the Wallabies were traditionally their weakest opponents, Australia's Class of 1989 proved they were a vintage selection when they went on to lift the World Cup, at Twickenham, two years later.

Along with their most significant tour to Australia, the Lions also broke other new ground in 1989 with sportswear manufacturer Umbro supplying 103 jerseys and other kit with an estimated retail value of £30,000 in exchange for "maximum brand exposure whenever possible".

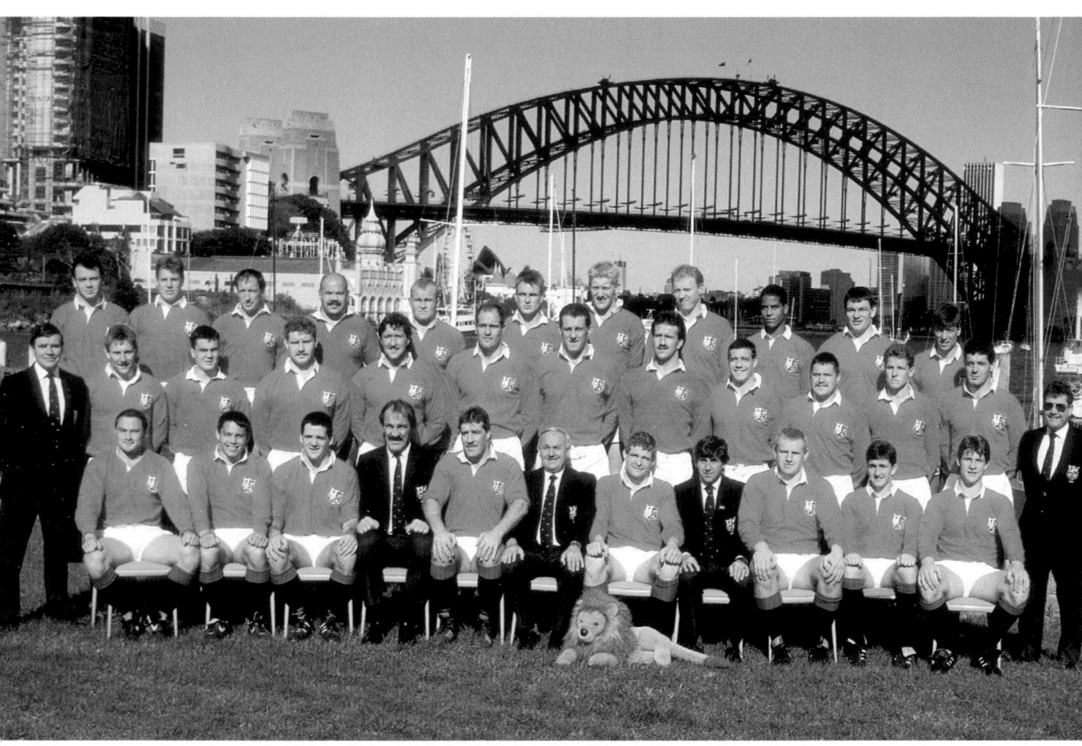

▲ The Lions on tour in Australia in 1989.

Inevitably the 1989 tour was the shortest in the Lions' history, as they played just 12 matches including the three Tests.

The 1989 team had to make history to win the series as no Lions side had returned home triumphant after losing the first Test, and lose it they did, 30-12 in Sydney.

With a margin that big and Australia in the process of developing a special team that would go on and win the

▲ The Lions front row.

▶ Lineout action from the third Test match against Australia in 1989.

1991 World Cup, there looked to be no way back for Finlay Calder's Lions, who were coached by Ian McGeechan.

Beaten to the victory by the Australian forwards, in the first Test, the Lions – after winning their first six tour games – were blown away conceding four tries, and scoring none.

But they got their trip back on track with a great midweek performance. Losing 21-11 to the ACT at half-time they roared back to win 41-25 and gave themselves an unexpected fillip going into the second Test, in Brisbane.

The feel-good factor carried them into the trip to Brisbane, and with five changes to the Test team they were ferocious in their pursuit of victory, keeping the series alive with a 19-12 win.

Punch-ups punctuated the Test as the Lions refused to be intimidated, relying as well on a tactical kicking masterclass from half-backs Rob Andrew and Robert Jones.

The Lions showed their backbone, after being 12-6 down at half-time they scored tries from Gavin Hastings and Jeremy Guscott to take the series to the deciding Test, back in Sydney.

The final game was settled by a startling error from the man who was so often the nemesis of British rugby; David Campese. The wing threw a hopeful pass to Wallaby full-back Greg Martin, which went loose allowing Ieuan Evans to dive on it.

Evans's second half try took the Lions into a lead they never lost, and although penalties from Michael Lynagh closed the gap to one point, the Lions held on for an historic 19-18 victory.

Bizarrely two games were staged after the final Test, the Lions beating both NSW Country and an ANZAC XV, which included three New Zealanders.

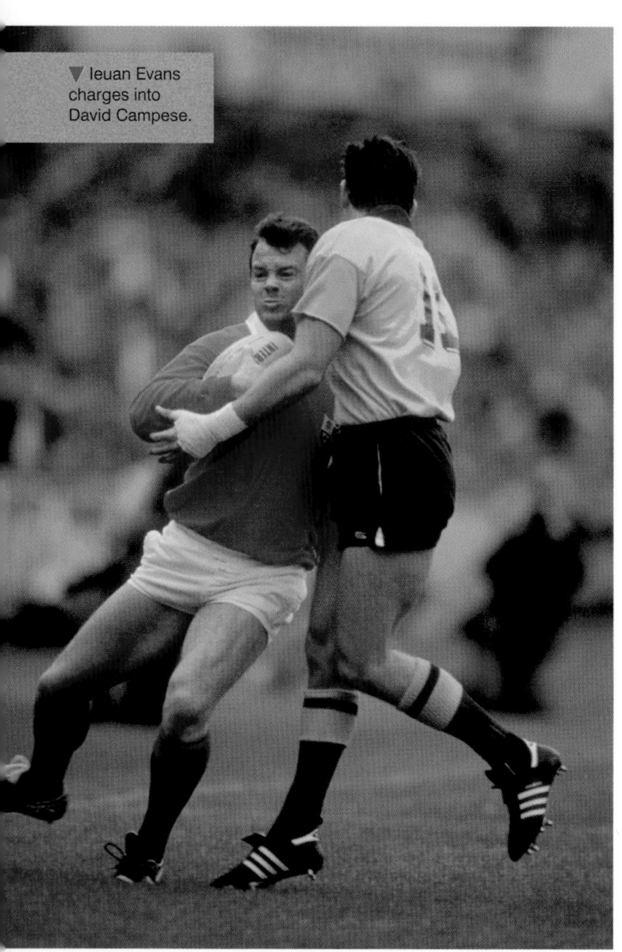

▼ Ieuan Evans charges into David Campese.

After failing to win a Test series since 1974, the 1989 Lions rejuvenated the shirt and all that the Lions side stood for.

The series had an undercurrent of violence that spilled over a number of times during the three Test matches and prompted captain Calder to comment on the attitude required for a British side to win Down Under.

"The large part of Australian life is sport, winning is everything," said Calder. "However, when it comes to playing anything against the 'Poms', we should never underestimate the undercurrent of their hatred towards their ancestry and, having played against them on several occasions, the explosive situations that occurred only highlighted that feeling.

"To the credit of the Lions, despite provocation both physical and verbal, the series was settled by tremendous commitment and team spirit."

A British and Irish side travelled to Paris later in 1989 to play France, in a celebration of the forming of the French Republic 200 years earlier, but as several leading players, including Calder, refused to play, it wasn't considered an official match.

Cast as the "Last of the

Amateurs" the **1993** Lions made the trip to New Zealand two years before the International Rugby Board declared the game of rugby union "open" or professional.

Coached again by Ian McGeechan, the first time anyone had coached the side twice, the Lions came agonisingly close to their second series win in New Zealand, following the legends of 1971.

The question of McGeechan's captain was hotly poured over,

▲ Robert Jones passes the ball during the Lions tour to Australia in 1989.

▲ Paul Ackford wrestles with Tim Gavin of the Anzacs during the 1989 tour Down Under.

▶ Ieuan Evans rounds Eroni Clarke to score in the match against Auckland, 1993.

especially outside rugby circles, as he plumped for Gavin Hastings, a star in 1989 over England's Will Carling who had led his side to Grand Slams in 1991 and 1992.

McGeechan's decision was shown to be correct later in the tour when an out of form Carling was dropped from the Test team, and when Hastings proceeded to break a series of Lions records on the tour. Hastings finished the trip with more Test points than any other before him (66); more points in a Test match (18) and most penalties (12) in a series.

The 1993 tour was also the last with more than a week between Test matches as the Lions became squeezed in an ever-increasing rugby calendar,

that was bringing more and more international matches, and of course a World Cup.

Hastings's record-breaking haul wasn't enough to give the Lions the elusive two Test victories but the quality of this side was shown in the way they fought back after losing the first Test, in Christchurch, 20-18.

In the pack, the Lions had the outstanding Ben Clarke, one player that New Zealand famously asked to be left

behind at the end of the tour!

Clarke and the Lions' finest day came in the second Test, in Wellington, where they racked up their record win against New Zealand, 20-7, Rory Underwood stunning the hosts with a 50-yard run and try.

They did it with 11 Englishmen in their side – Jeremy Guscott, Underwood, Rob Andrew, Dewi Morris, Brian Moore, Jason Leonard, Martin Johnson, Martin Bayfield, Clarke, Peter Winterbottom and Dean Richards.

The victory ensured that the 1993 Lions earned the respect of New Zealand rugby, not something achieved by every Lions side to arrive there.

Laurie Mains, who coached the All Blacks to their 2-1 win in 1993, even compared them favourably with the Lions who triumphed in 1971.

Mains said: "They had better match-winners in '71 but the '93 vintage are a more rounded and experienced side. What you also have to remember about 1971 is that New Zealand were in decline with a lot of players at the end of their careers.

"It may be that they do lack speed in certain areas but with their big ball-winning pack they have the ability to

play the game at the pace they want."

The 1993 Lions were unable to build on their victory in the second Test losing the third, in Auckland, 30-13.

The trappings of professionalism were in evidence on this trip. Umbro may have supplied the team kit in 1989, but in 1993, the Nike logo appeared on the jersey for the first time, Adidas taking over in 1997, in a deal that encompassed the 2009 trip to South Africa.

▲ Gavin Hastings is tackled by Grant Fox.

◀ John Kirwan tries to evade Scott Gibbs and Rob Andrew .

▲ Ieaun Evans charges forward.

The 1993 tour delighted the New Zealanders on and off the pitch, the home nation winning the series and the All Blacks making gross record profits of almost £2million, more than half of it from gate receipts from the trip.

Eddie Tonks, New Zealand's chairman said: "There is nothing to compare with a Lions tour. The public clamour to see them has never been greater. We will do everything we can to ensure this is not the last tour. I don't know how we would manage without them. There's no doubt that the players want the Lions to continue."

Luckily for Tonks and New Zealand, the Lions powered on, returning in 2005, and never looking in stronger shape despite their 3-0 series defeat when they came back, 12 years later.

▼ Ben Clarke on the attack against North Auckland.

The First Professionals

▶ The victorious 1997 Lions.

Many people, England captain Will Carling included, thought there would be no place for the Lions in the new professional era. The Lions, it was said, were the property of an amateur era when the Corinthian spirit of rugby was more important than winning and losing. But how wrong Carling and others would prove to be as professionalism meant an unprecedented expansion of the Lions. As the game became more about balance sheets and bottom lines, the Lions became even more treasured, the game's biggest brand.

Their place in the hearts of a new generation of British and Irish rugby fans was ensured in **1997**, when they travelled, without huge expectation to play the world champion South Africans. They emerged victorious from an epic series, 2-1, which was as brutal as it was electrifying.

The game went open and the Lions went from strength to strength under Martin Johnson.

1997 South Africa
Captain: *Martin Johnson*
Test Matches: *Won 2-1*

The victory was built in the management team of coach Ian McGeechan, his assistant Jim Telfer and the wily old manager Fran Cotton.

All three of them were steeped in the history of the Lions and their first inspired choice was that of their captain – a little heralded (at the time!) second row from Leicester, Martin Johnson.

McGeechan said he wanted the 6ft 7in Johnson because of his imposing stature. He knew the Springboks

Kohler
SCOTTISH PROVIDENT
adidas

presented the most intense physical challenge of any side in the rugby world and in Johnson he had a formidable character at the helm of the team.

McGeechan also had the insight to tap into the rugby league players who were returning to union, after the game became professional in 1995. McGeechan fast-tracked six former rugby league players into the squad and they were crucial in the series victory as the coach promoted both the Test team and midweek side equally.

The tour was the first to cost more than £1 million to stage, so the Lions went in search of their first shirt sponsor, finding Scottish Provident, who paid a reported £400,000 for the privilege of becoming the first company to have their names on the famous red jerseys.

The Lions were the rank outsiders. The 1993 team had lost in New Zealand and South Africa had gone on to lift the World Cup.

But the Lions upset the odds in the most sensational way, winning the first and second Tests, before South Africa chalked up their first victory in the dead rubber of the final Test.

Johnson's Lions earned the right to

go into the first Test, in Cape Town, with an excellent chance, after winning seven out of their eight provincial matches beforehand.

And even after losing to Northern Transvaal 35-30 in the fifth game, they plotted their course back into the tour through their midweek team who won a close fought contest with Gauteng 20-14 and then against the Emerging Springboks, just before the first Test.

Coach McGeechan's tactic of placing huge emphasis on his midweek team helped the Lions move into the first Test in confident mood.

But in the end it took a piece of brilliance from England scrum-half Matt Dawson, who only got his chance due to an injury to Rob Howley.

Dawson picked up the ball from

▲ Simon Shaw crashes over to score in Welkom during the 1997 Lions tour of South Africa.

◀ The trophy won by the Lions on their 1997 tour of South Africa.

the base of a scrum 20 metres out and dummied the South Africa defence not once, but twice, to charge home unopposed.

The victory in the second Test, which clinched the series couldn't have been more dramatic.

With the scores locked at 15-15, with three minutes to go, centre Jeremy Guscott slotted a drop goal through the posts to give the Lions their first series win in South Africa since 1974.

"This is a lifetime memory," Guscott admitted. "I hit it just right and it sailed through. Somebody had to do it, so it might as well have been me.

"I only had one thing on my mind – to drop a goal. Then I thought 'What if I miss this and we lose the match?' But the kick sailed through the posts. The Test series is ours. Thank you very much."

South Africa scored three tries in the second Test, to all kicks from the Lions, who sealed a hard fought win with a rearguard action that made their captain proud.

Johnson said: "I can't really believe it – it is a credit to every one of the squad. It was a hugely tense atmosphere, and everybody involved in this tour can feel rightly proud.

"No one gave us a chance when we got here, but we've done it and it's fantastic. Everyone said we were there for the taking, but how wrong could they be.

"They came at us with so much pride and we kept them out. We knew that if we were close with 10 minutes to go, we would win."

◀ Jeremy Guscott, the hero in the second Test.

▼ John Bentley, one of the finds of the trip, streaks clear to score against Emerging Springboks.

The Lions win was built on their unrelenting defence, but South Africa's inability to take their chances in the second Test, with the boot was also significant, as acknowledged by Bob Dwyer, the former Australia coach.

"In the second half I was convinced that the Lions had gone," said Dwyer

◀ Martin Johnson avoids a tackle during the tour match against Western Province, 1997.

in *The Sunday Times*. "They defended superbly, just as they had done in Cape Town. They had a lot of defending to do and they never shirked the job.

"You have got to kick your goals and the fact that South Africa kicked none from six attempts (three penalty goals and three conversions) was obviously a crucial factor. They never had a shot at goal after the 24th minute of the match which means that for three-quarters of the game the Lions defence did not concede a penalty in a kickable position; an extraordinary statistic.

"My men of the tour would be Ian McGeechan and Jim Telfer, the coaches. The improvement shown by the players in their ability to play a fast-paced game was remarkable, as was the change in their body positions and the leg drive of the team collectively. You have to put those factors down to the coaching. The pair's leadership and technical expertise have been almost without peer and nobody should ignore their huge contribution to this series win."

The third Test, in Johannesburg was a match too far for the Lions. Of course, in the run-up to the game they talked well about wanting to make it 3-0, but they had won the series already and few were surprised when the South Africans earned some pride from the tour with a 35-16 victory, which failed to dampen any of the Lions' celebrations.

4
adidas
ntl:
adidas
ntl:
adidas
ntl:
adidas
ntl:
adidas

Lions In The New Millennium

At the start of the new Millennium it was a case of conflicting fortunes for the British and Irish Lions. They suffered two losses but in completely different circumstances, first losing an unforgettable series to Australia in the last match of the tour in **2001**, and four years later being hammered by a record margin in New Zealand.

The Lions moved into a decade stronger than ever, but started it with two defeats.

2001 Australia
Captain: *Martin Johnson*
Test Matches: *Lost 2-1*

2005 New Zealand
Captain: *Brian O'Driscoll*
Test Matches: *Lost 3-0*

In 2001 the Lions broke new ground. Not only did Martin Johnson become the first player to captain the Lions on two different Lions tours, they also employed a foreign coach, in Graham Henry, for the first time and he took the biggest party, of 37 players, which turned into 44 with the injuries.

For New Zealander, Henry, it was a case of near, but yet so far as his side won the first Test in Brisbane, only to lose the next two in Melbourne and Sydney.

The second professional Lions were paid the handsome sum of £15,000 when selected for the tour, and would have been handed a £7,000 bonus if they had ended the tour unbeaten, and won the Test series.

In the end, the 2001 Lions were unable to overcome a mounting injury list and it became the difference

◀ The Lions pack get their orders from skipper Martin Johnson.

▶ Martin Johnson and Neil Back combine to tackle Toutai Kefu.

between winning and losing.

The side was barely able to stage a training session in the last week of the tour, as they had so many casualties. Players like Lawrence Dallaglio, Dan Luger, Phil Greening and Mike Catt were selected but failed to make the first Test, while others like Richard Hill and scrum-half Rob Howley failed to finish the Test series. Hill, the man never dropped by Sir Clive Woodward in his England days was the biggest loss, along with Dallaglio.

"We suffered many injuries and some of the boys were held together with sticky tape by the time we started the last Test," admitted captain Johnson, after the Lions lost their first series in Australia in their history.

"They were running on empty. We gave it our all but just came up short, it's as simple as that."

The Lions performed superbly outside of the Tests, kicking off with a 116-10 victory over Western Australia in Perth, although they did lose to an Australia A team in Gosford, 28-25, before beating New South Wales and New South Wales Country in the run-up to the Tests.

An exciting series came down to the final 40 minutes of the final game on the tour as the Wallabies triumphed 29-23 in Sydney to take the series 2-1.

A titanic third-Test decider was sealed through 19 points from full-back Matt Burke and two Daniel Herbert tries in front of 84,000 fans at the Olympic Stadium.

"The number of people I spoke to were trying to be supportive and said what a wonderful tour it has been, how much they have enjoyed the rugby and how much they have respected the people on the field giving 100 per cent," said coach Henry.

"I guess that you've got to look at the bigger picture and say there are a lot of positives to come out of it."

Henry said that if future Lions teams were to be successful they needed to look at the structure of the tours, with most emphasis being put on the Test matches.

Henry added: "In the professional era the whole structure needs to be looked at. If you are going to play a tour of this intensity at the end of the domestic season you will have to look at more time between matches. Players need more time to recover. It is a question of whether you can afford to play so many

midweek matches."

A somewhat divided tour didn't help Henry. Many in the midweek side were less than committed while two English players – Matt Dawson and Austin Healey – vented their frustration in newspaper columns that threatened the unity of the party.

With Donal Lenihan, who famously led the midweek side to Australia in 1989 installed as manager, the Lions moved into the new decade as a sporting phenomenon with more than 20,000 fans leaving Britain and Ireland to follow them.

Those fans were treated to one of the great occasions in the first Test in Brisbane, when the Lions upset the odds with a 29-13 win that woke up the world champions to the huge challenge that the Lions can mount.

It took the Lions less than two minutes of that first Test for Jason Robinson to score a stunning try, standing up and going around Chris Latham with an incredible burst of speed.

The Lions left Brisbane that day thinking the series was in their grasp, but it was the only Test match they would win on the tour.

The **2005** tour to New Zealand will be remembered for all the wrong reasons, by Lions fans at least, as the side suffered record defeats in all three Tests, hammered the length and breadth of the north and south islands.

The tour got off to an awful start, even before the players left Britain

◀ Martin Corry wins lineout ball against Australia.

▼ Rob Henderson is tackled by Elton Flatley.

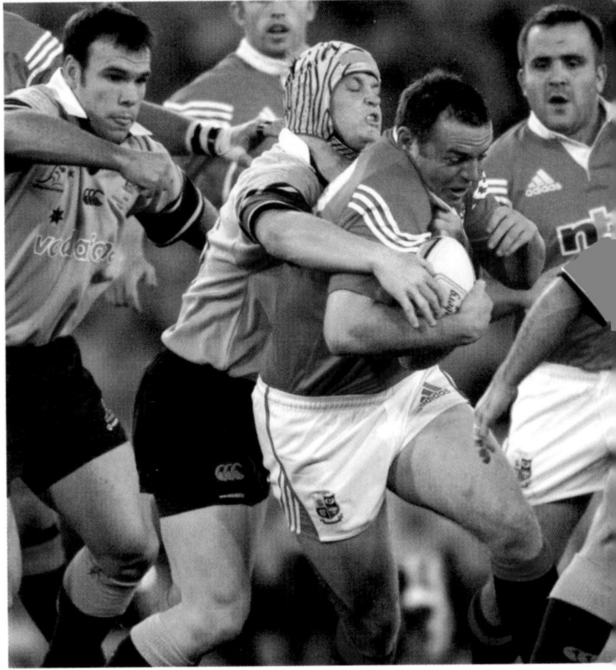

▲ Andrew Walker is hauled down by Lions' Jason Robinson.

▶ The Australians try to stop Martin Corry.

and Ireland. Sir Clive Woodward had assembled the biggest squad in the history of the Lions (44 players) and he agreed to a warm-up game in Cardiff, against Argentina, before the side departed, to help balance the books.

As it turned out the Lions came within a Jonny Wilkinson kick of losing to Los Pumas, playing like a group of individuals, rather than a team, and they never regained the momentum lost at the Millennium Stadium.

The Argentina Test was later confirmed as a Test match, with caps awarded by the Lions.

The Lions management have pledged never to repeat many of the innovations brought in by Woodward. They would never take so many players with them again, never play a warm-up game and ensure the midweek team and the Saturday (or Test) side wouldn't be split into two separate teams as they were under Woodward.

The former England coach, who led his side to World Cup victory two years earlier, set down his plan to beat New Zealand and the Lions committee fell in behind him.

Woodward had revelled in his "chief executive" role with the England team, making decisions on and off the pitch, and although the Lions granted his every wish, including the appointment of arch spin doctor Alastair Campbell to head his media team, the tour was the worst – in results terms – in the history of the Lions. Woodward's influence over the 2005 tour even led to him commissioning an "anthem" called *The Power of Four* especially for the 2005 tour to New Zealand. Neil Myers composed the tune, and the piece was performed for the first time in public by Welsh opera singer Katherine Jenkins before the Lions match against Argentina. The anthem was never adopted by the supporters and was dropped by the time plans were in place for the 2009 trip.

Hammered from one end of New Zealand to the other they conceded a staggering 107 points in the three Test matches.

Woodward believed the Lions should be split into midweek and Saturday (or Test) sides and to that end he picked more players than ever before (44) and had separate coaching teams for each side. The policy failed as it left disgruntled players and morale low.

Woodward was also criticised for relying too heavily on the England players who won the World Cup for him in 2003. Even though Wales won a Grand Slam in 2005, Woodward picked only 10 Welshmen and 20 England players.

Woodward wasn't helped on the field by a succession of injuries, two

▲ Lions captain Brian O'Driscoll leads his team out at Christchurch, New Zealand.

▶ Tana Umaga, the All Black captain powers through to score a try.

crucial ones coming in the first quarter of the first Test match.

Lawrence Dallaglio dislocated and broke his ankle in the first match, against Bay of Plenty, and then both captain, Brian O'Driscoll and key man Richard Hill were injured in that first Test in Christchurch.

O'Driscoll's injury left the bitterest taste as it came in the second minute of the match and resulted from him being dumped on his shoulder by All Blacks captain Tana Umaga and hooker Keven Mealamu. O'Driscoll himself called it "a cheap shot".

With these three great players on the field, the Lions may still not have beaten a vintage All Blacks side, but without them the series victory was a formality.

The Lions even lost the game billed as the "fourth Test", against the New Zealand Maori, suffering a 19-13 defeat, their first victory in six Lions matches dating back to 1930.

After O'Driscoll's injury the captaincy was handed to Gareth Thomas, the Welshman doing much to unify the squad, but not even his charismatic personality could muster a Test win, even though he scored the opening try in the Wellington Test, before the All Blacks roared back, Dan Carter claiming 33 points in the 48-18 win.

The only success came for the midweek side, who won all their games, completing their 100 per cent record with a 17-13 victory over Auckland, but in truth that set of results reflected the standard of the teams New Zealand sides put out in the midweek games.

Woodward's Lions ended their tour

with seven wins in 12 games and their first whitewash in the Tests for 22 years.

But Woodward preferred to credit the All Blacks, rather than blame his own side for the defeats.

"We gave everything but New Zealand's skill levels are above ours and I think the better team won in the end," said Woodward.

"We are disappointed – we came out to win the Test series so we have failed. It's actually been a successful tour, and has been great experience.

"The Lions are very special. We've tried to uphold Lions' traditions but the game has moved

▶ Rico Gear fends off Dwayne Peel in the third and final match played at Eden Park.

▼ Lions player Brian O'Driscoll is caught between Wellington's Tane Tu'ipulotu and Jimmy Gopperth.

on and we were up against the best side in the world," he added.

"It's hard when you pick up the injuries we did, including some big names.

"Getting a team together so quickly has been difficult and it has been difficult to get momentum going on this tour.

"This has been one of the most challenging things I've done. The Lions are different. It's not like coaching a national team when you can build things. You have to try and do something special in a few weeks. There are not many things I would change. We've lost, and I accept that."

Some questioned whether the Lions had a future in the age of professionalism and the Rugby World Cup. But the popular support given to the 1997 and 2001 tours put an end to these questions.

The 2005 tour to New Zealand proved to be an even bigger event with a reported 30,000 fans travelling to follow the team.

In the years before the 2005 tour, the Lions Trust was founded as the Official Charitable Trust of the British & Irish Lions.

Its broad aim is to help the Lions' former players in need of assistance and to help further the development of the game as a whole, as well as assisting with community projects in the countries visited by the Lions.

Some of the money raised has already been put to good use, by way of assistance to some former Lions who have experienced some form of hardship through ill health, finances or other problems and via the four Home Unions' own charitable trusts.

adidas

The Next Destination

▶ Ian McGeechan, the Lions tour head coach.

▶▶ The new Lions shirt for the 2009 tour.

Since 1891 the Lions have won 16 Tests against the Springboks and lost 21, while seven Tests have been drawn.

It will be a case of going back to their roots for the British and Irish Lions in South Africa. After a 2005 tour to New Zealand that featured the end of many of the traditions that made the Lions great, the 2009 tour will invoke much of the history of the side.

As happened in 1997 and 2001 the Lions will once again take on the current world champions, after the Springboks beat England in the 2007 final, in Paris.

And in another comparison with 1997 the Lions committee have gone back to the coach they employed 12 years ago, Ian McGeechan, to lead this tour.

McGeechan is the archetypal Lion. A superb player on tours in the 1970s, the 2009 tour will be his fifth as a coach.

If anyone embodies the spirit of the Lions it is McGeechan and that's why the tour will be in safe hands.

Sir Clive Woodward's trip in 2005 tried to break new ground but McGeechan's trip will be more of a traditional affair.

Gone will be the Lions song brought in by Woodward, the separate coaching teams for the midweek and Saturday sides and the squad will be reduced to 35.

"We'll do everything together," said McGeechan. "We'll always train together as the players must believe that each and every one of them has as much chance as the next of playing in the Test matches.

"Even on Test-match mornings, if we have a session for those who aren't involved, it will be run by the usual coaches. Every player will have the same opportunity to state his case for Test selection."

They certainly don't travel to South Africa with history on their side as the Lions have one Test series victory in nine meetings with the Tri-Nations sides, of course under McGeechan in 1997, but the difficulty of pulling four nations together, into one team, has

▶ The Loftus Versfeld Stadium which will be one of the venues during the 2009 Lions tour.

never been more acute than in the professional era.

The Lions are always judged by their performance in the Test matches, but McGeechan is obsessed with the way the midweek team will perform, as so many times he has seen the spirit and emotion in the side playing on a Tuesday or Wednesday translating into the momentum that allowed the side on Saturday to win.

"I still think about Donal Lenihan in 1989 on the tour to Australia. There was real purpose to the midweek team he led," McGeechan said.

"In that side there were players who probably knew they weren't going to play Test-match rugby, but, gee, he made that midweek experience special. The nature of the Lions means that you should always have a good Test side, but the environment they work under can be very different, and that is set by the midweek group."

McGeechan has already begun his forensic examination of South Africa, watching them beat England, Wales and Scotland in the autumn of 2008.

"I was impressed with their patience. I don't think they try too much too early. They have tremendous composure," said McGeechan.

"They don't dive in and take themselves out of the game. They don't make unforced errors. They're just very patient. But when they get a turnover or an opportunity everyone gets excited. That's what impressed me about them.

"In terms of building my own team, I'm looking at how well players deal with pressure. You want the guy who doesn't make mistakes. He might not be the fantastic, eye-catching individual people are talking about occasionally, because what you need is consistency of performance. And then you put somebody alongside him who is doing the same, and then somebody else alongside the both of them, and soon you're beginning to construct something that will begin to challenge South Africa at Test-match level. It's not about unearthing a super-tactic. It's about the ability to keep delivering the basics under pressure.

"When you face South Africa, it's your pack that sets the tone, and that's the best place to lead the side from. If there isn't an obvious captain there I won't force one, but that is my preference. It's also about how we want

to come across as a group.

"There is a huge responsibility on the Lions simply because of the numbers that follow them, and I want people to think more of the Lions badge after we have returned home. That's the ultimate plus of being a Lion. It's that other people want to put the jersey on when there is a Test match coming up because of what we represent.

"I still think people don't understand the pressure of playing in a Lions Test series. It's as much pressure as a World Cup final because you are against opponents who regard you as the biggest challenge they can ever face, and you are operating in their country over a protracted period. On

▶ The newly constructed Nelson Mandela Bay Stadium in Port Elizabeth.

top of that, the history of the Lions demonstrates that we don't always get it right. Four successful tours in 130 years is all that we have managed.

British and Irish Lions tour to South Africa, 2009:

Saturday May 30: *Highveld XV, Royal Bafokeng*

Wednesday June 3: *Golden Lions, Ellis Park*

Saturday June 6: *Cheetahs, Vodacom Park*

Wednesday June 10: *Sharks, ABSA Park*

Saturday June 13: *Western Province, Newlands*

Tuesday June 16: *Coastal XV, Port Elizabeth*

Saturday June 20: *First Test, ABSA Park, Durban*

Tuesday June 23: *Emerging Springboks, Newlands*

Saturday June 27: *Second Test, Loftus Versfeld, Pretoria*

Saturday July 4: *Third Test, Ellis Park, Johannesburg*

Other books also available:

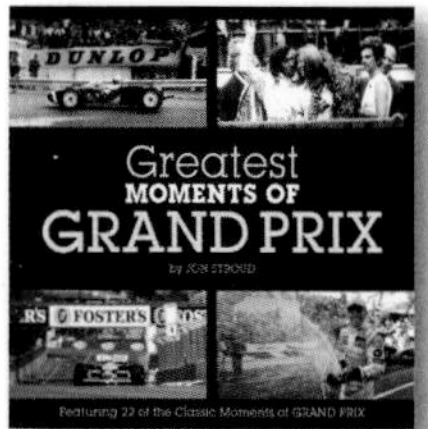

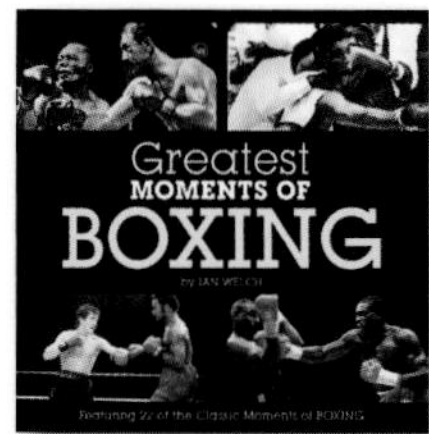

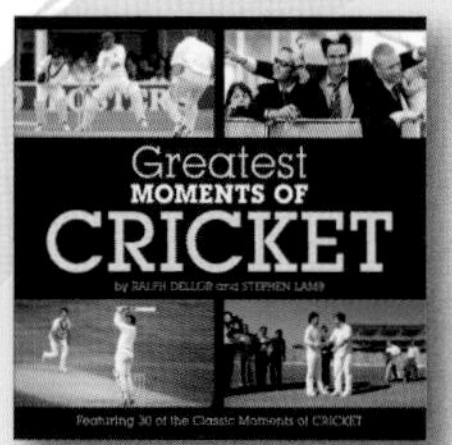

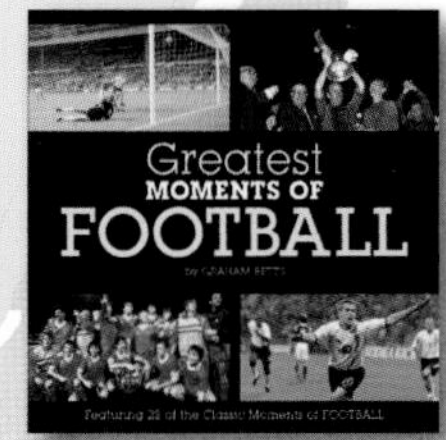

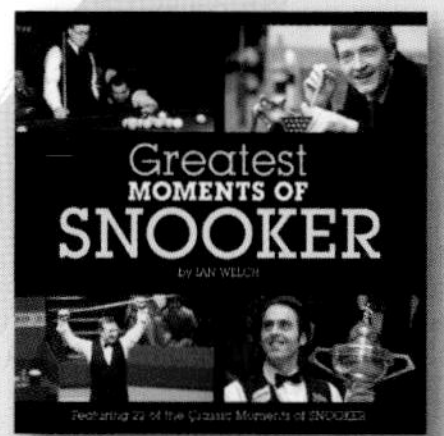

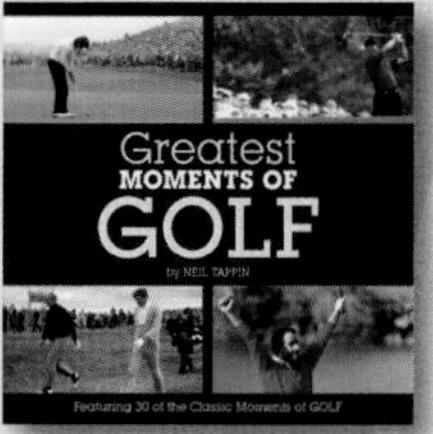

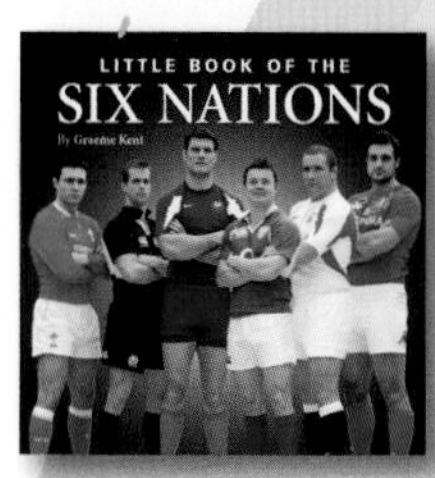

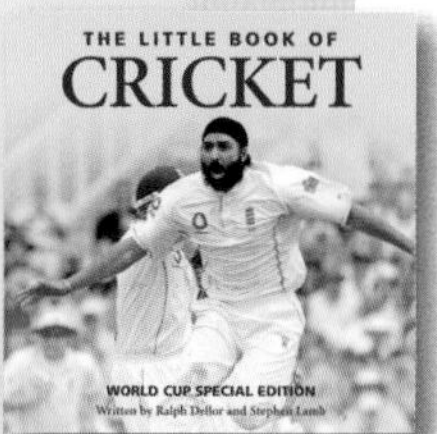

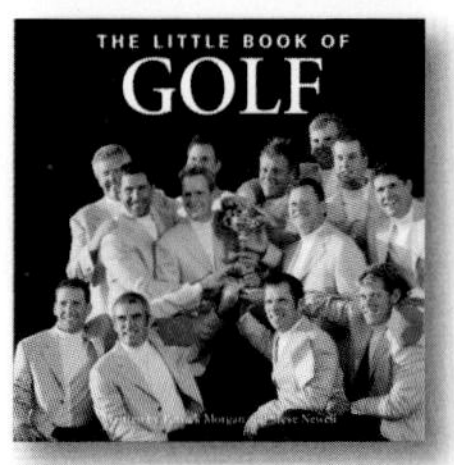

Available from all major stockists

The pictures in this book were provided courtesy of the following:

GETTY IMAGES
101 Bayham Street, London NW1 0AG

Creative Director: Kevin Gardner

Design and Artwork: David Wildish

Picture research: Ellie Charleston

Published by Green Umbrella Publishing

Publishers Jules Gammond and Vanessa Gardner

Written by Paul Morgan